Behaviour

Management

in the Classroom

Behaviour

Management

in the Classroom

A Transactional Analysis approach

SANDRA NEWELL AND DAVID JEFFERY

David Fulton Publishers
London

David Fulton Publishers Ltd
Ormond House, 26–27 Boswell Street, London WC1N 3JZ
www.fultonpublishers.co.uk

First published in Great Britain by David Fulton Publishers 2002

British Library Cataloguing in Publication Data
A catalogue record for this book is available from the British Library.

ISBN 1–85346–826–6

This book is dedicated to all hard-working teachers everywhere and
to all those pupils who have at some time felt misunderstood

Typeset by Elite Typesetting Techniques, Eastleigh, Hampshire
Printed in Great Britain by The Cromwell Press Ltd, Trowbridge, Wilts.

Contents

Foreword		vii
Preface		ix
About the Authors		xi
Acknowledgements		xiii
List of Figures		xiv
Introduction		xv
Part 1	What is Transactional Analysis?	1
	1 Introduction to Transactional Analysis	3
	2 Philosophical Assumptions in TA	5
	3 Life Positions	8
Part 2	Developing Relationships in the Classroom	11
	4 Moving Individual Pupils to the OK Position	12
	5 Moving Groups of Pupils to the OK Position	17
	6 Strokes	21
	7 Contracts	30
	8 Role Modelling	37
	9 Ego States	49
	10 Transactions	58
	11 Relationships	64
Part 3	Structuring the Lesson	69
	12 Time Structuring	70
	13 The Start of the Lesson	75
	14 The Middle of the Lesson	79
	15 The End of the Lesson	81
Part 4	Maintaining Relationships in the Classroom	83
	16 Life Scripts	84
	17 Games	93
	18 Discounting	103
	19 Winners and Losers	107
	20 Punishments	120

Part 5   Staying OK   125

                21 How Teachers Can Stay OK   126

                22 Conclusion   129

Appendices   131

Glossary of TA Terminology   136

Further Reading   139

Bibliography   141

Foreword

Learning is a necessity for our development from birth to death: our survival depends upon the accumulation of knowledge. This process begins with our parents in whose lives we are placed. As we grow and mature we learn from many sources, not least from our teachers and educators. Without the capacity of our seniors to sustain a relationship with us, based upon care, respect and acknowledgement, we cannot engage in that creative process, in a happy way.

Maintaining human bonds and working connections is not easy: all our relationships present us with emotional and intellectual difficulties. Often we are not taught or shown how to resolve our anger, distress and fears in early life. For a teacher leading a group of up to 35 children these unresolved, raw but natural feelings can often turn into behaviours, in the pupil and teacher, that can escalate into conflict.

Transactional Analysis is a beautiful theory, giving us a way of psychologically understanding ourselves and others. It also provides a framework for human interaction and the maintenance of social bonds.

This book is an impressive document; it communicates the theory in an effective way and addresses the number one concern of any teacher I know: that of discipline.

Discipline conjures up images of control, order and even punishment. However, what teachers and educators are really promoting are social cohesion and self-responsibility and the maintenance of the working group, however large or small.

Teachers and those being taught all have psychological needs of stimulation, recognition and structure (*What Do You Say After You Say Hello?* (Berne 1991)). Often definitions are based upon the perceived needs of the class but teachers have needs too. Their emotional, intellectual and physical satisfaction is often ignored, leaving them drained, frustrated and perhaps negative about their experience in the classroom, which can be a lonely and uncomfortable place.

Sandra Newell and David Jeffery define the learning process as a mutual responsibility of the whole group and encourage teachers to look at their own behaviour as well as that of their pupils. It is not uncommon for all of us, when under stress, to be more inclined to want to blame and often punish when things get difficult. This makes the problem not ours and certainly not ours to solve.

This book is a reflection of two open, warm, loving, motivated and highly effective thoughtful teachers with experience and passion for their work. With their easy use of Transactional Analysis this book is a wonderful combination of support, reassurance, help and learning.

My ten-year-old son defines his happiness at school in terms of his teacher's warmth and compassion, my two-year-old daughter is sitting on my knee and is yet to begin her life at school. I hope for them that they have met and will meet people like Sandra and David – teachers are really important in the happiness of children and of us all.

Carol Lucas, BEd (Hons), Certified Transactional Analyst (Psychotherapy), Provisional Teaching and Supervising Transactional Analyst, UK Council for Psychotherapy registered, Director of Therapeia South Manchester Centre for Psychotherapy, Co-Director of northwesttraining

Preface

This book came about as a result of many conversations we had about school. It was very often on a Friday evening about 6 o'clock when we put on some background music and sat down together to enjoy a glass (or two!) of wine. We would sit and discuss incidents involving individual pupils or whole groups that had occurred during the week and how we had dealt with them, what had worked and what had not.

When we had both had some Transactional Analysis (TA) training, we started to realise that the techniques and strategies we were using tied in very well with the concepts in TA and then used these more and more in managing conflict. Many a time we said: 'We really should write all this down for other teachers to use.' However, we never really thought that we would actually get down to doing it. We did, and this book is a summary of our conversations.

We have modelled the book on the kind of personal development books which we ourselves find interesting and useful. Each chapter tends to start with a quote, something which can easily be remembered and which is concise.

We have then explained some aspects of Transactional Analysis theory. Our aim is not to explain the whole of the theory in depth, but merely to pick out the key concepts in order to familiarise the reader with the main ideas.

Throughout the book, we have used capital letters for the TA concepts. We have used the word 'pupils', rather than 'students', in order to emphasise the difference between pupils in the classroom and student teachers. When referring to the teacher or the pupil, we have used the pronoun 'they' to avoid either being sexist or using the somewhat cumbersome 's/he'.

This explanation of the theory is followed by examples of how the theory might manifest itself in pupils' or teachers' behaviour. These are types of behaviour, which are easily recognisable. We have also included activities based on questions to focus the readers' minds on their own thoughts, feelings and behaviour and the kinds of situations they may find themselves in with pupils.

We hope that we have provided lots of practical suggestions and examples as to how the theory can be used to positive effect in the classroom in order to turn conflict into collaboration.

About the Authors

Sandra Newell taught in Shropshire for 19 years in three 11–16 comprehensive schools. She started her career at Meole Brace School in Shrewsbury, where she taught for five years. She was Head of Languages at Fitzalan School in Oswestry for two years and was then appointed to the post of Head of Languages at the newly formed Marches School in Oswestry, an amalgamation of the former Croeswylan and Fitzalan schools, where she taught for 12 years. She is currently Course Leader for the PGCE Modern Foreign Languages course at University College Worcester.

David Jeffery has taught in a variety of schools in Shropshire and Telford and Wrekin for 23 years. He started his career at Belvidere Boys' School and Monkmoor Girls' School, where he taught for four years. He then moved to Telford, where he taught both in Hollinswood Middle School and in Stirchley Upper School. He is currently Head of History/Humanities at the Lord Silkin School, an 11–16 comprehensive school in Stirchley, Telford.

Both authors have been involved in taking responsibility for the pastoral care of pupils, either as Head of House (Sandra) or as Acting Head of Year (David) They have delivered in-service training to teachers, both in their own schools and in county. These have involved the topics of anti-racism, library and study skills, managing behaviour and assessment.

David has been involved in the project Discipline for Learning in his school and Sandra was involved in the RAISE Project (Raising Achievement in Shropshire Education), which looked, in particular, at the achievements and attitudes of boys.

In addition, both have attended training courses for fostering/adopting special needs children. The course included sections on abuse, HIV and AIDS and a considerable amount of time was spent on managing behaviour, conflict and anger.

They have both gained a Certificate in Counselling and have completed three years training in Transactional Analysis Psychotherapy.

Acknowledgements

There are many people that we need to thank for their help in bringing this book together. These are people who have given us their ideas and suggestions or their support.

We would like to thank the following people:

All the teachers we have ever worked with and all the pupils we have ever taught

Carol Lucas and Jim Davis for their excellent Transactional Analysis training

Our families and friends

Sandra's PGCE students

The RAISE committee at the Marches School

Diana Pringle, Sandra's therapist

Trudi and David Newton for their help with TA diagrams

Roger Day and Francesca Hannah of TA UK

Robin Fryer of the ITAA

Dr Dusay and Dr Karpman for their permission to use their diagrams

Jude Bowen, our Commissioning Editor

Alan Worth, the Production Manager

Eric Berne for starting the whole TA thing!

And, of course, last but not least, each other.

List of Figures

9.1   Ego States: structural model
9.2   Ego States: functional model
9.3   Example of an Egogram
9.4   Your own Egogram
10.1   A complementary transaction
10.2   A crossed transaction
10.3   An ulterior transaction
17.1   The Drama Triangle

Introduction

Have you just taught the group from hell? The group every other teacher in the staff room knows or is relieved not to be teaching? The group that makes you feel angry, frustrated and helpless? The group that

- never listens
- is always talking instead of listening to instructions
- never does any activity quietly
- constantly fidgets
- fiddles with anything on or under the desk
- annoys each other by name calling
- finds everything 'boring'
- loses their books
- never has any equipment and never gives equipment back
- draws on the materials that you have worked hard to produce.

Do some of these problems seem familiar? Are you feeling tense and stressed by the mere mention of these characteristics?

When student teachers embark on a teacher-training course, the area that concerns them most is behaviour management. How can they get the pupils to behave? In addition, many experienced teachers have sleepless nights worrying about this issue, or dreams in which a class runs riot. After all, this is a case of one individual asserting their authority and control over a class of up to 35 pupils. It can be a lonely and frightening position.

This book explores the relationship between the theories of Transactional Analysis and Behaviour Management (discipline). In the book, we offer practical strategies and solutions to these behavioural problems. We have found the techniques to be extremely useful and effective in our combined 40 years of teaching and we hope that they will help you in the same way, whether you are a trainee teacher, newly qualified teacher, experienced teacher or, indeed, a parent. Not all of the ideas in this book will suit your style. You might take some of these ideas and use them or adapt them to your own circumstances. 'There is no one correct way of teaching ... Every teacher is an individual and brings something of their own unique personality into the job ... An effective, reflective teacher is one who can integrate theory with practice' (Capel *et al.*, 1999).

Throughout the book it is recognised that the following play a vital role in managing behaviour in the classroom:

- well-planned and carefully organised lessons
- defined learning outcomes which are communicated to pupils
- clear explanations and examples
- effective questioning
- a variety of activities which match the ability and maturity of the pupils
- activities which are challenging and interesting
- high expectations
- pace
- colourful and interesting resources.

There are no magic solutions to some difficult groups and both authors are or have been teachers who still have 'bad discipline' days. However, the strategies we offer you in this book have helped us to realise that we are not helpless in the face of bad behaviour. There are things that we can do that help us to create the learning atmosphere we want in our classrooms.

We believe that prevention, negotiation and compromise are better alternatives than continually arguing with pupils. Bad behaviour must never be ignored, but it does not always need to be confronted in an aggressive manner. Teaching is about forming a relationship with pupils and the ideas in this book aim to help you develop and maintain a relationship with even the most badly behaved pupils.

It should not be forgotten that pupils in secondary schools in particular are going through a difficult period of their life when:

- they grow beyond their parenting relationships
- they develop their own personal philosophy of life
- they deal with sexual changes and develop as a sexually mature person
- they find and develop a place among grown-ups.

(Levin, 1988)

This can lead to challenging behaviour as they work through adolescence.

Discipline does not need to be something that is negative, nor something that is imposed. Discipline is part of learning; it helps learning to take place. In fact, the word 'discipline' itself actually means 'to teach' or 'to train'. However, both of us can remember not learning at school because the discipline was so harsh and humiliating it made us too fearful to learn. Discipline can be defined as 'The practice of care and respect towards others and towards self' (Humphreys, 1998).

It is important that pupils are also given the opportunity to develop their emotional intelligence as well as their academic intelligence. Howard Gardner (1993) outlines seven different types of intelligence. These include interpersonal (relationships with others) and intrapersonal (self-awareness) skills. Education should teach pupils how to have their needs met, while at the same time respecting the needs and rights of other people. This will also help them to become responsible members of the society outside of school. The model we offer could be modified and developed as part of either a Citizenship or Personal and Social Education Course.

Finally, discipline, especially self-discipline, can be a creative part of the learning process in the classroom. It can be the very thing that helps to unlock a child's potential for learning.

Part 1

What is Transactional Analysis?

Chapter 1

Introduction to Transactional Analysis

'Transactional Analysis is a theory of personality and a systematic psychotherapy for personal growth and change.' This is the definition used by the International Transactional Analysis Association (ITAA). The term Transactional Analysis (TA) was first coined in 1958. Its originator was Eric Berne (1910–70). He worked in psychiatry and psychoanalysis in post War America and began writing at the end of 1956. His ideas form the basic framework of TA. His school of TA is referred to as 'Classical TA'. In the early 1950s, Berne held regular clinical seminars in San Francisco and he and his colleagues formed the ITAA.

Since then, many other writers have expanded on his original theories. There are, however, two other main schools of TA: Jacqui Schiff developed Passivity Theory, which is known as the 'Cathexis' school; and Robert and Mary Goulding developed the 'Redecision' school of TA. TA has proved to be successful in a wide variety of applications. It is used in the treatment of all types of psychological disorders, from everyday problems (such as in the classroom!) to severe psychosis.

It has four main areas of application: Counselling, Psychotherapy, Educational, Organisational. The basic theory used is the same, but there is a difference in emphasis and in techniques. In this book, we do not intend to go into depth about the theory, but rather to take the basic concepts used in TA and apply them to the classroom situation.

TA offers

- a theory of personality (using a three-part model known as the 'ego-state model')
- a theory of communication or interpersonal behaviour (using the ideas of transactions)
- a theory of child development (using the idea of a life script).

The key ideas in TA which we shall discuss in the chapters of this book are:

- Life Positions
- Strokes
- Contracts
- Ego States
- Transactions

- Life Scripts
- Games
- Discounting.

If you are interested in learning more about TA, please refer to the Bibliography and Further Reading List at the end of the book.

Chapter 2
Philosophical Assumptions in TA

The following three philosophical assumptions underlie the theory of TA:

- People are OK.
- Everyone has the capacity to think.
- People decide their own destiny and these decisions can be changed.

These are optimistic assumptions and empower the individual. Let's take each one and see how it applies to the classroom.

ASSUMPTION 1: PEOPLE ARE OK

What does being 'OK' mean in terms of the pupil? It is often easier to define what is not OK behaviour in the classroom. Pupils who behave badly are often not OK with themselves and do not get on with other pupils. They may be the pupils who are:

- bullies or name callers
- aggressive
- hyperactive
- unable to work with other pupils or share materials
- passive or victims
- withdrawing loners who find it difficult to get on with other pupils
- fearful, stressful pupils
- painfully self-conscious.

This creates a picture of a pupil who is not OK: a pupil who disrupts the lesson, shouts out, irritates other pupils and does not get on with their work, or is too fearful to perform well. In this case, their *behaviour* is not OK, but Berne would argue that the *essence* of the pupil is OK. This is when it is powerful to say to a pupil, 'I like you, but I am not happy with the way you are behaving.' It may sound like a cliché, but it separates the pupil from their behaviour and leaves them with some self-esteem. They can change their behaviour, but they cannot change who they are. These types of behaviour may not necessarily stop other pupils from working, but they do have a limiting effect on the pupils' own progress. Behaviour which is not OK stops learning and does not resolve conflict fairly.

Pupils who feel OK about themselves often

- have a healthy respect for themselves and others
- are aware of their behaviour and have a sense of fairness
- are aware of the needs of others and will accept other pupils' ideas, share materials and apologise when necessary
- have an ability to encourage, praise and help other pupils
- have the confidence to try out new things
- show a desire to do their best
- are assertive, rather than aggressive.

Pupils who display these types of behaviour are likely to develop well both as learners and as people. OK behaviour helps to provide learning opportunities and experiences. It promotes collaboration.

What does being 'OK' mean in terms of the teacher? A piece of informal research undertaken by Sandra with some pupils as part of the RAISE project brought together characteristics which pupils look for in a good teacher. These were as follows:

- firm but fair
- not biased
- respects pupils
- is a good role model
- works hard
- gets involved
- takes an interest in the pupils as individuals
- is patient and calm
- is willing to listen
- understands and cares
- has a good personality
- is enthusiastic
- has a good sense of humour
- treats pupils as human beings
- is never sarcastic
- never puts you down.

It is interesting to note that not one of these is about the work done in the classroom. They are all about the way the teacher treats the pupils.

ASSUMPTION 2: EVERYONE HAS THE CAPACITY TO THINK

TA believes that everybody (except people with severe brain damage) has the ability to think. In the classroom, pupils have the capacity to think about their behaviour and take responsibility for it. In some cases they need to be encouraged to think about what they are doing or have done. Likewise, the teacher has the capacity to reflect on the situation or position in which they find themselves in the classroom or with a particular group.

ASSUMPTION 3: PEOPLE DECIDE THEIR OWN DESTINY AND THESE DECISIONS CAN BE CHANGED

Whenever a pupil or teacher makes a decision, that decision can always be changed. People can change. If pupils and teachers think about their actions and take responsibility for them, they can then move towards actively changing them. Teachers can facilitate these changes by encouraging pupils to think about their behaviour, offering pupils choices and making them aware of the consequences of the various choices.

Chapter 3
Life Positions

... one's basic beliefs about self and others, which are used to justify decisions and behaviour.

(Steiner, 1974)

Berne believed that a child 'has certain convictions about himself and the people around him'. In other words, from early childhood, pupils develop fixed ideas about themselves and other people, as a result of the way that they have been treated in their family. TA calls these ideas or convictions 'Life Positions'. There are four Life Positions:

1. I'm OK, you're OK
    This is the position that is most healthy and the one teachers should aim to promote because this Life Position will help to create a relationship of mutual respect. Conflict is also less likely. Pupils who adopt this position consider themselves valued and respect other people.

2. I'm OK, you're not OK
    Teachers who adopt this position will not show respect for pupils. Conflict is likely to develop because pupils will be aware of this. The teacher may blame the pupils for everything that goes wrong in the classroom and be unprepared to change their own behaviour in order to improve the situation. Pupils who adopt this position will be over-critical and may accuse the teacher of picking on them.

3. I'm not OK, you're OK
    Teachers adopting this position are likely to be highly self-critical and convinced that they are not doing a good job. They may underestimate their own ability, while promoting that of other colleagues. Pupils adopting this position are likely to be withdrawn, consider themselves stupid or useless and put themselves down all the time. They may also experience shame and in this 'down' position, they are unlikely to learn.

4. I'm not OK, you're not OK
    This is the most negative Life Position, both for teachers and for pupils. Teachers are self-critical and are negative towards pupils. Pupils put themselves down and blame teachers for their lack of success.

The ideal position in the classroom is to move towards a position where the teacher is OK and the pupils are OK. This will create a good working environment which promotes self-esteem for all people concerned. The teacher needs to use strategies that will help pupils to develop improved self-esteem. It will be difficult to develop positive relationships with pupils unless the teacher can move troublesome pupils towards the 'I'm OK, you're OK' Life Position.

ACTIVITY

Look at these examples. What Life Positions have these pupils chosen?

Brian: 'I am hopeless at Maths. I will never be able to work this out unless you [the teacher] help me.

Jane: I can't do this and you [the teacher] never help me.

Paula: Mr Jones showed me how to do this. I did well in his class. He was a good teacher. I understood him; all you do is confuse me.

Patrick: I enjoy this subject because you make it interesting.

ACTIVITY

Think about the last time that you lost an argument. How did you feel? How did you feel the last time that you were criticised? Which Life Position did you choose? How easy was it to continue to have a relationship with the person who upset you?

It is important that the teacher deals with situations fairly and respectfully and does not use humour or sarcasm to belittle or humiliate students. Teachers must aim to put a full stop at the end of any problem as quickly as possible and move themselves into the healthy position of 'I'm OK' as a teacher and help the pupils to get to the position of 'we are OK' as pupils.

One way of doing this is by being specific about the behaviour you do not like and refraining from criticising the pupil. 'I do not like it when you write on my work sheets' (This behaviour is not OK). 'I think you are a nice person who knows that is wrong' (You are still OK). Compare this to: 'You must be a stupid idiot to write on my sheets.' The teacher thus attacks the pupil and the behaviour. The pupil will forget about the writing on the sheets and start to defend himself and argue. 'I'm not stupid. Your sheets are stupid and so is your work. It's boring.' As we will see in a later chapter, this approach has escalated the problem and leads to a 'Game'. The pupil has moved from: 'I'm not OK, you possibly are OK' to 'I'm OK, you as teacher are definitely not OK.'

You also need to emphasise that as a teacher, as an educator you are interested in teaching and not punishing. You make pupils clear about your role. You are offering them a service. You make the pupil aware that they may still have options. Allow them to retreat with dignity and lose face gracefully. Create a 'we all win' situation.

ACTIVITY

Think about someone who treated you unfairly or rudely. Did they allow you to retreat with dignity? What are your feelings about this person? Could you still cooperate with this person? Would you do your best for this person? How could this person have resolved the situation so that you felt OK?

'The overall philosophy of TA begins with an assumption that we are all OK. This philosophy leads to what is probably the most basic assumption of TA theory and practice – I'm OK and You're OK' (Woollams and Brown, 1978).

Part 2

Developing Relationships in the Classroom

Chapter 4

Moving Individual Pupils to the OK Position

In the following chapters, we aim to explain how individual pupils can be moved from a 'Not OK' to an 'OK' position. However, let us first of all give an overview of how this might be achieved.

Here are some steps that a teacher can take in the classroom in order to help a pupil to become OK or stay OK. Underpinning all these ideas and strategies is the importance of the relationship between teachers and their pupils.

1. Praise pupils and reward good behaviour (Chapter 6, Strokes).
2. Make the rules of the classroom explicit and make pupils partners in the learning process (Chapter 7, Contracts).
3. Model good behaviour and appropriate ways of expressing feelings (Chapter 8, Role Modelling).
4. Use clear, unambiguous communication (Chapters 9 and 10, Ego States and Transactions).
5. Develop relationships (Chapter 11, Relationships).
6. Structure time and lessons effectively (Chapters 12–15, Time Structuring).
7. Understand the influence of the pupils' family backgrounds (Chapter 16, Life Scripts).
8. Help pupils to get their needs met without being manipulative (Chapter 17, Games).
9. Challenge pupils' unwillingness to take responsibility for their actions (Chapter 18, Discounting).
10. Show forgiveness (Chapter 19, Winners and Losers).
11. Encourage pupils to change their behaviour (Chapter 20, Punishments).
12. Stay OK (Chapter 21, Staying OK).

Let us look at each of these in a little more detail.

1. PRAISE PUPILS AND REWARD GOOD BEHAVIOUR

Everybody wants attention. If pupils do not get attention through good behaviour, they will resort to bad behaviour to get noticed. Indeed, it is much quicker to get attention with bad behaviour! 'Children quickly learn that displeasing is also a way to get attention, and it often works quicker and more reliably than pleasing does' (Huber, 2000). If teachers give pupils attention, showing an interest in them as people, not just as pupils in their lessons, they will help to move the pupils to an OK position.

Bad (not OK) behaviour can be minimised by openly rewarding good (OK) behaviour. Pupils love praise, even if they say they don't! Praise also helps to develop self-esteem and a feeling of being OK.

2. MAKE THE RULES OF THE CLASSROOM EXPLICIT AND MAKE PUPILS PARTNERS IN THE LEARNING PROCESS

Pupils feel safer when there is structure. They need to know what is expected of them and what they can expect from the teacher. This needs to be explicit. At times, this might almost sound like a 'running commentary', particularly at the beginning, but it is vital in setting out what OK behaviour involves. In addition, pupils are more likely to behave and work well if they are given an opportunity to take ownership of any ground rules or intended learning outcomes, thereby involving them in their own learning process.

3. MODEL GOOD BEHAVIOUR AND APPROPRIATE WAYS OF EXPRESSING FEELINGS

Unless a teacher models OK behaviour, a pupil may not know how they should behave. The teacher should model how to behave as a learner, how to treat other people and how conflict can be avoided or resolved.

Teachers making requests should always do so politely, they should apologise if they make a mistake and be a good role model in terms of how they treat other people, both in the classroom and around the school. By so doing, they model OK behaviour, giving pupils the opportunity to imitate.

Some pupils have extremely difficult home backgrounds. Inevitably this can affect their behaviour in class. When challenged, feelings may arise which may feel out of their control, such as anger. It is important that the teacher acknowledges these feelings and allows the pupil to express them in a safe and appropriate way. Again, this gives both teachers and pupils the opportunity to move towards being OK.

4. USE CLEAR, UNAMBIGUOUS COMMUNICATION

Berne firmly believed that the relationship between himself and his clients should involve open, honest communication. In this way, he could ensure that the client had full knowledge and information about what was happening. This ties in with the philosophical assumptions that people are OK and have the capacity to think. Indeed, he also suggested that ideas should be expressed simply enough for an eight-year-old child to understand them. The theories of TA are therefore expressed in simple terms so that they are not confusing.

The idea of clear communication with learning outcomes, ground rules, ideas, instructions and explanations expressed overtly and in simple terms is extremely useful in the classroom. It encourages pupils to communicate clearly and creates a safe, trusting environment, where pupils and teachers can be OK. It is important too that teachers choose the correct way of responding to pupils, either by their tone of voice or by the content of what they say in order to minimise or avoid (an escalation of) conflict. Teachers need to keep the lines of communication open and ensure that what they say is justifiable. They should not keep 'secrets' about what is expected or what is going to happen.

It is important too to remember that every piece of behaviour is a form of communication. So if a pupil misbehaves, it is useful to ask ourselves what they are trying to communicate. '[C]hildren do not engage in unwanted behaviours to make life difficult for others. They do so because their fundamental rights have not been met … As a result they are forced into adopting actions which are "cries for help"' (Humphreys, 1998).

Finally, bearing the above in mind, teachers should remember not to take bad behaviour personally.

5. DEVELOPING RELATIONSHIPS

Teachers need to develop relationships with pupils that make themselves and the pupils feel OK. This means that they need to show an interest in the pupil, both as a learner and as an individual. Even if a pupil misbehaves, teachers should show that they believe that the pupil has the potential to change and be OK.

Relationships should be based on mutual respect. In such relationships, both pupils and teachers have their needs met and have an opportunity to show compassion and understanding towards each other.

6. STRUCTURE TIME AND LESSONS EFFECTIVELY

As mentioned before, pupils like structure. If they are not given a clear structure, they will quickly resort to bad behaviour. The teacher has a responsibility to do this clearly and effectively so that there is no 'dead time' when pupils can go off task.

7. UNDERSTAND THE INFLUENCE OF THE PUPILS' FAMILY BACKGROUNDS

The messages (verbal and non-verbal) which a pupil receives from their parents or primary caretakers in the first few years of their lives can set the tone for how they think, feel and behave for the rest of their lives. It is important that teachers recognise this, understand the influence that this can have and know how to deal with it.

8. HELP PUPILS TO GET THEIR NEEDS MET WITHOUT BEING MANIPULATIVE

Pupils will use various strategies to get what they want out of a situation in the classroom. They will adopt a familiar pattern of behaviour which generates discomfort for all those involved. Teachers can expose these patterns of behaviour and help the pupils to ask openly for what they want.

9. CHALLENGE PUPILS' UNWILLINGNESS TO TAKE RESPONSIBILITY FOR THEIR ACTIONS

Pupils often deny that they have done anything wrong, in other words, they 'discount' what they have done. The first step is therefore to get them to take responsibility for their actions by gently challenging them. Pupils need to understand that bad behaviour has consequences and that they have a choice whether to behave or misbehave.

10. SHOW FORGIVENESS

'Forgiveness does not mean we condone injustices of the past' (Kornfield, 2000). Given that the teacher's main aim is to move the pupil to the I'm OK, you're OK position, it is important not to get obsessed with punishing pupils. If punishment is a constant threat, it can force pupils into a corner. We need to ensure that pupils feel that they have been treated fairly. In addition, it is a good idea to start every lesson with a blank sheet, rather than carrying forward incidents from previous lessons.

11. ENCOURAGE PUPILS TO CHANGE THEIR BEHAVIOUR

This book advocates preventive approaches to disruptions which should minimise the necessity to punish pupils. If, however, there has to be some form of punishment, it should keep the pupil OK. It should not be about getting revenge, but should be geared towards change.

12. HOW TEACHERS CAN STAY OK

If teachers overwork and do not look after themselves properly, they will become tired and are more likely to snap at pupils and treat them unfairly. By staying OK, teachers will have more patience to deal with pupils and will therefore be modelling OK behaviour.

Chapter 5
Moving Groups of Pupils to the OK Position

We have seen the importance of moving individual pupils to the OK position and some ways in which the teacher can do this. Now let us look at how the teacher can move whole groups of pupils to the OK position. Thus creating an 'I'm OK, the class is OK' situation.

There will be days when the teacher will feel that they are OK but 9Z are not OK: '9Z, you are far too noisy'; '9Z, you have left the classroom in a real mess'; '9Z, your work today has been terrible.' However, the teacher should always look for any positive behaviour that can move the relationship from 'You are not OK as a class' to 'You are OK as a class': 'I have been impressed with the way you have worked quietly today'; 'I am really pleased with the way you have worked as a class'; 'Over the last week you have been coming into the classroom really sensibly.'

Much has been written about the dynamics of groups. In terms of TA, therapy can be done with individuals or with groups. In the classroom, we are dealing with groups all the time. It is useful therefore to look at some of the important issues surrounding the psychology behind groups which might affect the way individuals behave in the group or the way the group completes work together.

Groups are a kind of microcosm of life or society. Working with groups is very challenging because every person in the group has their own expectations about what that group might be like. Berne suggested that this was based on their earliest experiences of being in a group, i.e. the family.

ACTIVITY

Think of all the groups of which you are or have been a member. Pick out one good experience of being in a group and one bad experience. Write down what made those experiences good or bad. What was missing from the group where you had a bad experience?

Berne also felt that members of a group have a preoccupation with the leader of the group. This emphasises the important role which teachers play in managing classes.

Remember too that pupils very quickly make judgements about the person in front of them (the teacher). Many people say that pupils can recognise a teacher's fear and take advantage of it! Later in the book we will look at how the teacher can role model the behaviour they want.

The teacher is responsible for structuring time. 'Carelessness about time is considered to be destructive group leader behaviour' (Carol Lucas, 2000). They also have to set the ground rules for the group.

What do individuals want from a leader?

- boundaries
- potency
- careful time structuring
- sensitivity and compassion
- patience
- awareness
- assertiveness
- self-knowledge
- confidence
- creativity
- honesty
- skills
- good organisation
- a willingness to be close.

Again, the teacher can model all of these.

ACTIVITY

Which leadership skills do you have? Which ones need developing?

Berne felt that groups go through a series of developmental stages which are necessary, otherwise, ultimately no work will get done.

Tuckman (1965) identified four different stages of development in all groups:

- forming
- storming
- norming
- performing.

A fifth one was added later: adjourning. Let us look at each of these in turn and how they might relate to a group in the classroom.

FORMING

This is when the group first gets together. In the classroom, it could be a newly formed tutor group or teaching group. This is the point at which it is best for the teacher to define the boundaries, show that they are in charge and reassure pupils about their safety within the group.

STORMING

The group starts to get to know each other and the leader better and individual members may start to rebel. Psychologically this is about whether the leader is strong enough to give the pupils what they want and need and stand up to them. Teachers need to ensure at this point that they do not come across either as too fragile or as too frightening. Rebellion may be overt or aggressive or it may manifest itself through passive behaviour.

ACTIVITY

How do you rebel in groups? Do you compete with the leader, get angry, agitate, make faces, stand up to the leader or try to get the group to hurry up? What do you need from the leader at that time?

NORMING

Feeling safer within the group, having tested the boundaries, the group becomes a more cohesive unit and people are more willing to express personal opinions. Shared norms about how to behave are developed. The teacher's role at this stage is to support and encourage pupils in their learning and behaviour and demonstrate flexibility.

PERFORMING

When a teacher and a class have developed a relationship of mutual respect, the energy can then be channelled into achieving tasks and producing work rather than conflict. This is when the leader should praise pupils, giving positive comments. They may even give up leadership temporarily so that pupils come out to the front and present ideas or perform their work. The leader minimises their leadership and controlling role while at the same time maintaining safety.

ADJOURNING

This is about ending the group appropriately. Some teachers do not say goodbye to pupils nor tell them exactly when they are leaving. They avoid the intimacy which a 'good goodbye' can bring. It is important for the pupils that the teacher does this well. It shows that they consider the pupils' feelings and gives them a chance to say goodbye properly. This is best done by expressing sadness that the group is disbanding but enjoyment in what awaits them in the future.

According to Berne, the leader's (teacher's) tasks are as follows:

- to keep the boundaries intact (to keep reinforcing the rules)
- to keep the task intact (keep the pupils focused on their work and on task)
- to stay strong (to stay OK despite the rebellion).

A leader or, in this case, the teacher's good handling of the group will contribute to successful relationships and work being successfully completed.

Chapter 6

Strokes

...the fundamental unit of social action.

(Berne, 1984)

When people transact, interact or communicate, they signal recognition of each other and usually get recognition in return.

Activity

Think of the last time someone praised you. How did you feel? What effect did the praise have on you?

Teacher says, 'Tell me about one lesson in which you are doing well.' Pupil looks at teacher with a blank expression and gives a shrug of the shoulders. There is silence. The pupil in this example is not trying to be awkward or uncommunicative. They feel they are being honest. Such pupils will see themselves as not OK, they will feel deficient, inadequate, not good enough, a failure, etc.

Some pupils rebel against their feeling of inadequacy. They may feel that they are misunderstood or misjudged. These pupils may see their teachers as being not OK. The only time they can get any recognition is when they misbehave. Some badly behaved pupils hide their feelings of inadequacy from the rest of the class by showing off or not taking the work seriously.

In many classes there will be the 'invisible pupils'. They plod along, do what the teacher says and never get into trouble. These pupils never get noticed and therefore get little or no recognition.

One very immediate way a teacher can encourage pupils who have poor self-esteem or are not interested in their schoolwork is by giving them recognition. Too often pupils go through days, even weeks, of school without any recognition. Even pupils who are keen on their work and want to do well may have an inaccurate picture of how well they are doing. They may well underestimate their success. 'No matter how intelligent, attractive or talented you may be – to the degree you doubt your worthiness you tend to sabotage your efforts and undermine your relationships' (Millman, 1999). In all these examples the teacher could help the pupil to change their perception about themselves as learners by giving them more praise (recognition).

Berne saw Strokes as an important need. He underlined that people need physical and mental stimulation and he called this 'Stimulus hunger'. He pointed out that as we develop into adults, recognition becomes a substitute for physical contact. Berne called this 'Recognition hunger'. Other people can show us that they have recognised our existence by smiling, laughing, complimenting, frowning, or criticising us. People (including pupils and teachers!) need Strokes to be physically and psychologically well.

WHAT ARE STROKES?

There are several different types of Strokes. Non-verbal Strokes, for example, may be a smile, a frown, a wave or a nod. Verbal Strokes may range from just saying 'hello' to a full conversation. Positive Strokes (praise) make the person feel good and negative Strokes can be hurtful and painful. Conditional Strokes relate to what a person *does*. Unconditional Strokes are given for who or what a person *is*, rather than what they *do*. This is why advice on how to reprimand pupils suggests separating the person from the behaviour.

Here are some examples of different types of Strokes which may be used in the classroom:

positive conditional: 'That is a lovely piece of work.'

positive unconditional: 'You are a lovely pupil.'

negative conditional: 'This work is a disgrace.'

negative unconditional: 'What a nasty piece of work you are.'

ACTIVITY

Think of the kinds of Strokes you use or give to pupils in the classroom. Make a list of Strokes, non-verbal, verbal, positive, negative, conditional and unconditional which you have heard teachers use or have used yourself. Think about the likely effect that these Strokes may have on the pupil(s).

GIVING AND RECEIVING STROKES

It is interesting to note how people give and receive Strokes. You may like to try this exercise with a group of pupils or staff.

> **ACTIVITY**
>
> Take it in turns to give each other positive (whether conditional or unconditional) Strokes. How do people give the Strokes? (Were they truthful, did they look embarrassed, did they 'play safe'?) How do people receive the Strokes? (Did they dismiss them, did they 'water them down', did they distort them?)

Apart from accepting the Stroke and saying 'thank you', in a natural way, other reactions to Strokes are known as 'discounting' which we will deal with in Chapter 18.

Other types of Stroke are called 'marshmallow' or 'plastic' Strokes. These are given out liberally, but are insincere and 'counterfeit' Strokes which start off positive, but have a negative 'sting'.

> **ACTIVITY**
>
> Try to think of some examples of marshmallow and counterfeit Strokes. Think of how these would be received by pupils.

Attention (recognition) is a hunger. It is something that needs to be satisfied. We all want to be noticed. Most of us want to be noticed for the things we do well. However, we need to consider those pupils who have five or so hours in school of never doing well. They feel that if they cannot be noticed for good behaviour, then they might as well get noticed for being silly. In addition, they can then get some self-esteem from being noticed by their friends.

Such pupils will find it easier to get attention for behaving badly rather than cooperating with the teacher because getting attention for bad behaviour is immediate. The teacher will give them instant recognition. They may also not know how to get attention in a positive way. It might not be part of their home background; no one has modelled it for them. In a large family he or she who shouts, fights or manipulates better than others is the one who gets noticed.

It is also worth pointing out here that boys can be more attention-seeking than girls. Boys in particular enjoy showing off. They often like to be the centre of attention. So when you are thinking of activities, it is a good idea to think about whether you are giving boys an opportunity to get noticed for positive things. If you do not give them this attention or opportunity for attention, then there is a good chance that they will try to get it through disruptive behaviour.

In contrast, you might want to think about how much time and attention you give girls in your lesson. You may want to increase this by talking to quiet girls once the class is on task. Walking around and making sure they know that they are appreciated for their good effort, work or behaviour. Saying 'thank you' to them for working so hard at the end of the lesson as they leave the room may only take a few seconds.

In a discussion with pupils as part of the RAISE project, pupils bemoaned the lack of praise which they got in the classroom. They seemed to feel that praise was limited in some way and certainly felt that some teachers did not use the reward systems available to them appropriately or regularly.

ACTIVITY

How much praise do you give as a teacher? Make a subjective guess, think of a number out of ten. Do you tend to notice the negative things first?

Giving praise is a tiring activity. We often feel resentful; nobody gives me any praise. Why should I give these difficult pupils any praise? The problem with being negative is that what we give out has a habit of coming back. If you always start the lesson shouting at the students, they feel that you always have a go at them and you don't like them. Praise, on the other hand, builds up self-esteem.

Less able pupils will sometimes give in quickly or not even attempt to do a task if they perceive the work as being too difficult. They may fail themselves rather than face the threat of the teacher or their peers failing them. By using Strokes skilfully a teacher can help each individual or a whole class to feel that their contributions are worthwhile and valued. Obviously this does not involve the teacher giving lots of marshmallow Strokes. However, a teacher can find something about each pupil's work or behaviour that can be praised. For example, 'Neil, I like the way that you present your work'; 'Emma, you have lots of clever ideas'; or 'James, you are making more of an effort to understand ideas.'

The praise then becomes a vehicle for helping the pupil to move out of their comfort zone. Most of us are willing to try something new when we feel reasonably secure. Being aware of the need to give Strokes helps the teacher to concentrate on what positive things pupils do in their lessons. It makes the teacher more pro-active in using praise. The Strokes from the teacher help pupils to see themselves in a positive light, they are encouraged to focus on their strengths and not just on their weaknesses. The Strokes enable them to develop their own self-esteem. As their self-esteem develops, their feelings of security and worth increase. They are then more likely to try something new. For example, 'Neil, your work is presented well.' (The teacher regularly praises Neil about this aspect. He knows he is valued for this.) 'Is there a big idea in your work that you could tell us about?'

If the teacher normally asked Neil a question he might be silent. In this example, Neil may well attempt to answer the question because he has already been stroked for what he is good at. He feels that the teacher values him. With less able pupils the teacher can ask pupils in pairs to answer a question. This gives the less able pupils the security of not feeling stupid in front of the rest of the class.

Most pupils like to be liked. It is always important to underline that you like them, that they are OK but that, at times, their behaviour is not acceptable. However, there are some pupils, as we noted at the start of the chapter, who when asked to say something positive about themselves will look blankly back at the teacher. It is as if the teacher has asked them to describe what the surface of Mars was like. They have no idea of what they do well. This might be because no one has ever told them. They have heard plenty of times what they do wrong in a classroom. It might be to do with the way they see themselves, due to role modelling and messages given to them by their parents or others. These pupils need to be taught how to receive and give Strokes. Below are examples of how you might choose to do this in your classroom.

WAYS THE TEACHER CAN GIVE STROKES

First of all, it is important that pupils know in advance how they can get positive Strokes during a lesson. One way of doing this is to display posters around the room explaining the various rewards available and for what types of behaviour or work they are awarded.

Here is a list of possible ways in which the teacher can give positive Strokes

- Every lesson, reward pupils for good behaviour. Concentrate on the good behaviour rather than moaning at a class about how bad they are. For example, if a class is poor at getting their equipment out, praise and reward the pupils who do get their pens, pencil cases and books out ready for learning.
- Make cards on a number of things you value as a teacher (see examples in Appendix 3) – these might be for good behaviour, entering the room sensibly, completing all the work, presenting work neatly, etc. – and award cards to pupils.
- You can buy a stamp and go round pupils' books stamping good work and behaviour.
- Make a sheet with a number of things you want pupils to achieve. Each lesson, pupils nominate a card they want to gain.
- Each half-term, pupils who gain all cards get a letter sent home telling their parents how pleased you are with them (see Appendix 4).
- Make certificates for older pupils. For example, a certificate for year 10 for completing coursework. Give out the certificates in a formal setting, such as inviting a senior teacher or deputy head along to award them, or having them presented in assembly.
- Get pupils to write a behaviour target each lesson. My target today is to …
- Get pupils to identify something they are going to do to make the lesson more enjoyable. Get them to write it down in their books and at the end of the lesson get them to read them out. The teacher or the rest of the class can decide whether they have made the lesson better.

- Go around the class at the end of the lesson and ask the pupils to say how well they have worked out of 10. It is best to warn them in advance that you are going to do this.
- Get pupils to write in their books:
      Today Mr/Ms/Mrs … will be pleased with me because …
- Tell classes and individual pupils how pleased you are with their work or their behaviour.
- Go around a class and say something positive about each pupil. It is a good idea to have thought out your ideas first. Then see if any pupil in the class can remember the praise you gave to everyone. This makes a good memory game, pupils cooperate and most of all, they listen and remember the praise that you have given everyone.
- Choose something positive about a naughty pupil and praise them in private or public.
- Get the Head of Department, House Head, Deputy Head or Head to come and look at the books of a class you are proud of. Tell the member of senior management why you are pleased with the class.
- Get pupils to give a round of applause to other pupils who do things well.
- Tell pupils that clever thinking impresses you. Give out a 'big ideas' card.
- You can get pupils to produce Progress Awards: either give them a photocopied template that looks official and formal or get them to draw one out. On their certificate they will need to write down all the successful things they have done. With weaker groups, you will need to give them a list of things they might put on their award.
- Tell a less able class that they are presenting their work as well as a more able group.
- Use the word 'clever' in your class.
- Point out to the class when you see some good behaviour, work or impressive thinking.
- Tell a class how much you enjoyed marking their work.
- Send some pupils to show their books to members of the senior management team.
- If you go into another teacher's class and see a group that you teach – tell the teacher publicly in front of the class how much you enjoy teaching them.
- Underline to pupils that you will not stand for any bad behaviour that stops learning. You will go and see Heads of House etc. and complain about individuals but also underline that when people work well you will go out of your way to spread good news about them in school.
- If you have seen some good work of a class or an individual in another area of the school make sure you praise them for it.
- Tell the class that you have enjoyed a lesson because of their intelligence and their good behaviour.

- Get pupils to listen to a passage once. Then read the passage and get them to make notes. Praise the pupils who were able to write accurate and worthwhile notes. Give them a 'good listener' card.

It is also important to remember that the teacher can give written praise. In their written comments the teacher should always concentrate on what the pupil has done well. They can then give the pupil suggestions on how they can develop their work. The pupil can read the teacher's comment and respond to it. This opens up a dialogue about the pupil's work between the teacher and the pupil. Finally, the pupil can write a target note on how they can develop their work.

One of Sandra's PGCE students (Daniela Maurri) developed a very clever and unusual way of giving Strokes to a group made up mainly of low-achieving year 9 boys with poor self-esteem, attendance, punctuality and behaviour. Pupils were each given the name of a German football team and each lesson represented a match. During the lesson pupils were awarded points in 6 areas: attendance, punctuality, effort, participation, behaviour and classwork/homework. Pupils could only score one 'goal' in each area and in each game, there was a 'Man of the Match'. After three lessons, the person at the 'Top of the League' won a trophy which they kept for two weeks. Pupils received a yellow card for bad behaviour and three yellow cards over three matches resulted in a five point deduction. The league table was displayed in the classroom without pupil names on it, just the names of the teams (only the pupils in this group knew which team was which pupil). This worked really well with pupils gaining self-esteem, working much harder, showing enthusiasm and treating each other more fairly. They applauded each 'Man of the Match' and 'Top of the League' award.

WAYS OF GETTING PUPILS TO GIVE STROKES TO EACH OTHER

- Get two pupils to walk around the classroom and to look at other pupils' work. Emphasise to them that they cannot touch another pupil's book or equipment. They must write down any good work or behaviour that they see any pupil do. They can then report back to the class and pupils can be presented with cards.
- Get pupils at the back of the room to make a note of the pupils who are behaving well or who are working hard. They can comment on pupils and these pupils can be rewarded with a card, a stamp or round of applause.
- Have a 'big idea' challenge. Get pupils to write down three big ideas that everyone should have at the end of the lesson. Pupils can swap books. Have your big ideas in an envelope and at the end of the lesson a pupil can read them out and the pupils can check how many of the big ideas they got.
- You can have a 'Hot Seat'. Pupils come out and answer five questions about the lesson, which have been written by the class.
- Get pupils to revise a topic by playing 'Who Wants to be a Millionaire?' The pupils can write 15 questions, which should get progressively harder. Get them

to only offer one answer. You will make the alternative answers up if necessary. They can have a phone a friend, i.e. ask someone in the class. They can have an 'ask the class' option. You give the class alternatives and they vote by putting their hands up for the answer they think is correct. You can have a pretend certificate cheque for £1 million. These activities create fun and friendship between teacher and pupils.

- You can get pupils to make Progress Awards for each other.
- Get pupils to mark another pupil's work. Develop a marking scheme on the board and talk about feedback they can give. For example, they must say something positive and one idea about how the person could improve their work. Emphasise that you will not put up with pupils being rude or insensitive about another person's work. Talk about how pupils feel when a person is rude about their work. Share your own experiences.
- Get pupils to read their work and respond positively to it. Ask other pupils what they liked about the work.
- Get pupils to produce display work in a group. Develop a mark scheme with them. Put the display work up and get pupils to comment on what they thought was good about it. Get pupils to make a list of new ideas they learnt from it.
- Get another class to mark the display work and then read the positive comments to the class.
- Create a notice board where the pupils or the teacher can nominate the names of pupils in the class to go on the notice board. The teacher can cut out stars from card and the names of pupils and what they did well are written on these and stuck on the board. The teacher and the class might discuss what they want to call the board. There might be pupils who do not want their names put up on the board; this should be respected, but the pupils should be praised in other ways.
- Cut up some cards with positive comments on. Pupils can give each other a card. Pupils can then say which card they were pleased with.

THE STROKE ECONOMY

Claude Steiner (1971) believed that our parents give us messages, verbal or otherwise, conditional or unconditional about Stroking, which we take around with us as if they are ultimate truths, such as:

- Don't give Strokes when you have them to give.
- Don't ask for Strokes when you need them.
- Don't accept Strokes if you want them.
- Don't reject Strokes when you don't want them.
- Don't give yourself Strokes.

These also have implications for the classroom. It is often the case that when a school operates a system of rewards, there are some members of staff who do not use them. Pupils and teachers want feedback on their work but do not ask for it. Pupils and teachers sometimes reject Strokes even if they do want them. They may not be used to receiving them. Some teachers and pupils accept negative Strokes too readily.

There will be some pupils who will feel uneasy about accepting praise and will react more painfully to praise than they would do to a good telling off (see Life Scripts). It is important to be sensitive with these pupils and it might possibly be better to praise them on their own when other pupils are not around. They then get used to hearing praise from the teacher without feeling embarrassed or self-conscious. It becomes less easy for them to ignore or discount the praise.

Learning to give and receive Strokes is an important skill for a teacher to learn. There will be many teachers who are excellent at giving Strokes but never want or hear the Strokes that they are given. By accepting Strokes or asking for them, the teacher is helping themselves to maintain their own energy levels and is more likely to be able to operate from an I'm OK, you're OK Life Position.

Self-stroking is important. In the classroom teachers can often get dispirited, focus on the negative and forget all the good work they are doing. Saying to ourselves that we did something well or are pleased with the way things went is a positive affirmation which will help to improve our self-esteem. We should encourage pupils to do the same. Before a teacher marks a book they could ask a pupil the question: 'What do you like about your work?' The teacher can ask pupils, 'What do you do in this lesson that helps make the lesson pleasant for other people?'

The teacher can tell each pupil for homework to write down one or more things they like about their behaviour and work in the lesson. Next lesson the teacher can go around the class and pupils can say what they like about themselves. A variation of this is for the teacher to get the class working quietly and walk round and speak to pupils individually. If pupils struggle to come up with something, probably due to their own 'Stroke Economy', then the teacher could help them.

Praise helps the teacher to develop their relationship with both individuals and classes. It allows the pupils to feel they are valued. This then becomes a two-way process. Pupils feel valued; they then value the subject being taught because they feel they are gaining some recognition (success). The teacher feels that pupils are valuing them and their work.

Praise keeps group energy up. Nagging, telling off and shouting are wearing on both the teacher and the pupils. It drains everyone of energy. Praise opens up new possibilities. It helps everyone in the class to move towards personal growth and change and can be one of the most useful tools a teacher has for changing the behaviour of even the most disaffected pupils.

Chapter 7

Contracts

... an explicit bi-lateral commitment to a well defined course of action.
(Berne, quoted in Stewart and Joines, 1991)

... an adult commitment to oneself and/or someone else to make a change.
(James and Jongeward, 1996)

A contract is made based on open communication and it is the responsibility of each party to fulfil their part of the contract. It reinforces the TA assumptions that:

- People are OK.
- Everyone has the capacity to think.
- People can change.

In education, people often talk about 'SMART' targets. The same can be said of contracts in that they should be:

- **S**pecific
- **M**easurable
- **A**chievable
- **R**ealistic
- **T**ime-framed.

In addition, they should focus on the issue, situation or behaviour, rather than the person.

ACTIVITY

Look at these roles: parent, son, daughter, teacher, engineer, man, woman, husband, wife, Prime Minister.

Choose a role you feel comfortable with. Why is this role comfortable? Choose a role that is difficult to play. Why do you find this role difficult?

Some pupils find it difficult to play the role of a pupil in class. First, they do not know what the teacher expects of them. Second, no one has explained clearly what the role entails or modelled the role for them. Finally, they do not have a long-term view of education and seek instead instant gratification.

HOW CAN CONTRACTS HELP?

If we see learning as a shared experience, it is important that pupils understand what their role in the process is and how they can take responsibility for both their actions and learning. Don't all of us hate feeling powerless? Don't we feel angry when we feel insignificant and unheard? Contracts are a way of involving pupils in behaviour and making them feel that teachers do listen to them. They are also a way of helping them and guiding them from feeling 'I am not OK' and 'No one is OK' to a healthy position of 'I'm OK' and 'Other people are OK'. Contracts help pupils to know what is expected of them. They make them aware of their rights and responsibilities in the classroom. Contracts also make the pupils aware of the needs of both the teacher and other pupils.

HOW CAN A CONTRACT BE USED IN THE CLASSROOM?

Individual pupil contracts

If a pupil is constantly causing problems in your classroom, you can organise a time when you, your Head of Department, and the pupil can all sit down together in order to draw up a behaviour contract. Obviously it is sometimes difficult to find a time when you and your Head of Department are free or have the time to meet, however, the Head of Department can play the part of a witness and referee. When a pupil tries to wriggle out of their responsibility, it is useful to have a neutral person involved in the conflict to remind the pupil that they are creating a version of reality that never existed.

- Explain to the pupil how their behaviour is spoiling the lesson and stopping them and other pupils from learning. Be specific; explain clearly which behaviour is unacceptable.
- Explain in no more than two sentences simply and clearly how a Contract will help them.
- Work out with the pupil the things they can do to prevent this behaviour. For example: 'At present you are shouting out in lessons. What could you do differently?' (If the pupil struggles to come up with ideas, offer them suggestions.)
- Explore areas of conflict with the pupil and give them two or three targets that they must achieve each lesson.
- Talk about the benefits and the rewards of the Contract.
- Talk about the sanctions and the costs of the Contract.
- Underline that *they* will be making the choices. They must make the right choices.

- Ensure that the Contract is worded positively.
- Explain how long the Contract lasts. Give it a clear time frame.
- Get the pupil, the Head of Department and yourself to sign the document and date it.

If there is no time for someone to sit down with a pupil, you can give him or her a sheet with headings and they can write the information themselves. It is useful to experiment and be creative and develop your own Contracts to fit the particular pupils you are teaching.

CONTRACTS WITH WHOLE CLASSES

Teachers can develop more general Contracts with classes. How a Contract is built up depends on the class, your relationship with them and their ability.

- The teacher can discuss with a class expectations of behaviour, effort and the amount of learning that is to take place each lesson. Their expectations may be too low or unrealistic.
- Get pupils to write down the behaviour that will help lessons to be successful. The teacher can build up a list of behaviour on the board that will become the learning rules for the class. This could be formalised into a signed 'Agreement' (see Appendix 1, developed by Helen Pickford, a colleague of David's).
- What can pupils realistically expect from the teacher? For example, this might involve when disputes will be settled. Will it be at the end of the lesson? What rewards will there be? When will books be marked?
- The cost of achieving the Contract and the cost of not achieving it. What are the losses, benefits and outcomes? Benefits might involve, for example, certificates, a phone call or a letter home to a parent explaining how their son/daughter has improved their work and behaviour.

Pupils can make a page in their book look like a legal document; copy out the information and then sign it or the teacher can produce a word-processed document for them to stick in their books and sign (see Appendix 2). When there are problems, the teacher can refer to this document. How are pupils not keeping their side of the Contract? Obviously you, as the teacher, have to keep to your part of the agreement.

The Contract is something objective that the teacher can return to when pupils are trying to draw them into conflict about disruptive behaviour. The disagreement is not one of personalities but a case of the pupil not fulfilling their side of the Contract.

By making the pupils aware of the teacher's role and responsibilities in the classroom, the teacher is making sure they do not enter into games of 'Victim, Persecutor or Rescuer' (see Chapter 17). Contracts encourage pupils to be active and not passive. The problem with their behaviour or working habits is clearly identified and the way forward is indicated. They can no longer blame someone else for their behaviour. They have to learn to take responsibility for their actions.

However, changing behaviour is difficult and there may well be some problems before they modify their behaviour. Therefore there will be a need for the teacher to constantly look to affirm their better behaviour through praise and attention (see Chapter 6). The teacher might get the Contract out on occasions to praise the pupil and to remind them of how and why they are improving their behaviour.

WHAT ARE THE BENEFITS OF USING A CONTRACT?

- The teacher and pupils have a shared goal. Clear and positive outcomes are created.
- The pupils do not have to guess the rules.
- What the pupil has to do to be successful is clearly stated.
- Contracts encourage open communication. The teacher might ask the class or individual, 'How have we done today? Have we hit our targets and fulfilled our contract?'
- Contracts make it clear to pupils how they can get positive attention
- Contracts help to create a shared and safe learning experience.
- They stop pupils discounting and game playing. (See Chapters 17 and 18.)
- Contracts create something neutral to return to in times of conflict. They give a sense of fairness and justice.
- Contracts encourage teachers to adopt and model adult behaviour. The teacher cannot demand fairness unless they model it for the pupil (see Chapter 8 on Role Modelling).

CONTRACTS HELP PUPILS TO SET TARGETS AND GOALS

If a teacher is mentoring a pupil, they can use a Contract to help them understand clearly what they need to do to be successful. Contracts can be used to help pupils to develop specific skills. The teacher can explain the skill the pupils need to learn, the benefits of learning it and the commitment they need to make in order to be successful. Pupils do need to be made aware of the costs of being successful, which include the amount of study time, homework and attitude they will need to adopt. They can also be made aware of the benefits.

At the start of a Year 10 examination course, a teacher can develop a Contract with a class. The teacher can explain that the pupils are now young adults and they can only be successful if they fulfil their responsibilities. Pupils can be made aware of the need to do homework, keep notes up to date and complete coursework. They can be made aware of the benefits and the consequences of not fulfilling their side of the Contract. The teacher can make themselves and the pupils aware of what they are willing to do.

From this discussion, the pupil and teacher can develop a Contract that will, first of all, help the pupil to focus on what they want to achieve and, second, pinpoint the strategies they can use to achieve their goals.

Contracts can be useful in helping pupils to focus on the future. Some pupils wander through school with no sense of urgency or purpose. They waste their ability because they never look beyond the short term. The exercise below is useful for a tutor to do with their tutor group in Personal and Social Education lessons. The teacher might talk with an individual or a class in Year 9 about the benefits of fulfilling their potential. Pupils can then think about:

- their dream job
- a job that would be OK
- a job they would hate.

The teacher can get the pupil to imagine what they might achieve at the end of Year 11. This can involve skills, attitudes and qualifications. Questions on this might include:

- What qualities as a person have you developed?
- What do you like about yourself?
- What have you done well in?
- Why did you do well?
- Which examination results would you be disappointed in?
- How could these be improved?
- What will your future look like?
- What sort of career do you want?
- What will you need to do to make this happen?

Pupils can answer these questions and produce a Contract. They can get the teacher or another pupil to sign it and this can be reviewed in PSE lessons to see if they are making progress. This process teaches pupils to be reflective in their thinking. Finally teachers might want to develop Contracts for themselves (see Chapter 21 on how teachers can stay OK).

CONTRACTS FOR TEACHERS

Often teachers create stress for themselves by not breaking down a job into parts or they try to deal with everything without prioritising what has to be dealt with first. Also some teachers tend to go from one job to the next without either being aware of what they have achieved or celebrating their success. Therefore Contracts can be a means whereby teachers create awareness of what they want to achieve, how they aim to achieve it, the time/cost involved and, finally, some recognition of when they have achieved all or part of their Contract.

My contract

Class _____

What do I want to achieve? (Be realistic – are some targets short-term and others long-term?)

I want pupils on task more. (Long-term target over a school term.)

Target 1 – How can I achieve it? (Have I got the skills and resources?)
Making it clear to pupils on an OHT what work they need to complete during the lesson.

Making pupils aware during the lesson what they should have done and get pupils to come out to the front and tick off work they have completed.

Produce work for less able.

Get pupils to write a work target each lesson about how much work they must complete.

Reward pupils who complete work.

Give a 'pupil of the lesson' award.

Get pupils to check to see who has completed work.

Target 2
Reward pupils who put hands up.

Warn pupils of the consequences of shouting out – one warning and then moved to another seat, another warning and removed from the lesson.

Have a room/teacher organised that I can send pupils to who constantly shout out.

Pupils sent from the lesson will have to complete work either at break or at home.

(It is worth noting that in this section the teacher may have needed In Service Training in order to gain the skills and expertise needed to meet the targets.)

Cost of meeting my targets
I will need to produce work that less able can access. (Timescale: long-term – one evening a week.)

I will need to produce cards as rewards. (Timescale: short-term – weekend.)

I will need to organise for a teacher to accept pupils who are sent from my room for shouting out.

How will I know I have achieved my targets?
Target 1

I will be able to cover more work. Pupils will complete more work. Pupils' assessment marks will be better. There will be a more pleasant working atmosphere.

Target 2

There will be fewer interruptions and a better relationship between the class and me. Fewer pupils will need to be kept behind.

Benefit of meeting targets

I will be able to teach and enjoy the lesson.

Pupils will understand rewards and punishments. This will allow me to develop better relationships with the class.

I will be able to give more time and attention to those pupils who are behaving well.

I will feel more confident and secure because I have a clear plan for how to deal with the behavioural problems I have experienced with the class.

A Contract such as this encourages a teacher to be more consciously aware of what they are trying to achieve and how they are going to achieve it. It also encourages them to be reflective about their teaching and how they can improve their performance in the classroom. It stops a teacher from being passive. They can be active in changing things they do not like in their classroom. Finally, it is important that Contracts are worded positively. When therapists use TA techniques with clients, they ensure that their contract is for positive change. So, for example, instead of saying: 'I will not be aggressive', they are encouraged to say: 'I will be more calm and assertive'. A good way of summing up Contracts can be found in a book called *Getting to Yes* by Fisher and Ury. 'Successful negotiation requires being both firm and open' (Fisher and Ury, 1989).

Chapter 8

Role Modelling

WHY IS THERE A NEED FOR MODELLING?

Pupils do not pick up ideas about mathematics or any other subject out of thin air, they need the ideas taught to them and they need skills modelled for them. This is true of behaviour too. Teachers need consciously to teach and model fair and respectful behaviour.

Some pupils whom you teach may not have an adult in their life that models either politeness or ways of resolving conflict fairly. Their norm might be getting things by manipulating, sulking or being violent. These pupils need to be taught what OK behaviour is and they also need to learn how to widen their repertoire of positive behaviour. Some pupils need to learn what good behaviour looks and feels like before they can behave appropriately towards other people. In order to behave better, they need someone to model the behaviour that will help them develop both as good learners and as people.

WHAT DOES MODELLING INVOLVE?

A teacher needs to be clear and consistent about the type of behaviour that they want to model in their classroom. They then need to model this acceptable behaviour at every opportunity and reward the class for copying it. Pupils can also be encouraged to model good behaviour for each other.

The teacher has to set both an example and a standard of behaviour that the pupils must follow. One way a teacher can do this is by not demanding anything from their class that they are not prepared to do themselves. For example, the teacher does not borrow a pen or pencil from a pupil without asking permission. The teacher models a whole class attitude and policy to personal property. The pupils see that no one in the class has the right to touch any other person's property without permission.

Teachers can get pupils to reflect on what constitutes good behaviour by asking them questions. For example, they can give pupils choices of behaviour and then ask them which behaviour seemed to be helping the learning process.

Teachers can also model for pupils how to learn in a group by role playing good and bad behaviour and then asking the pupils to comment on the behaviour. The teacher can model bad behaviour and then ask pupils how this will cause conflict and prevent learning from happening. A teacher can draw the attention of the whole class to good class or individual behaviour. 'I really like the way this group of pupils sits down quietly and makes sure everything is laid out on their desks at the start of the lesson.' A class that has worked well and produced good work can show their work to another class and explain how they produced it. This allows pupils to see what good work looks like and to understand how good work is produced.

Another strategy teachers can use is to ask a badly behaved pupil and two other well-behaved pupils to sit at the back of a class and to write down during the lesson the names of pupils whom they think worked well. The pupils can have a couple of minutes at the end of the lesson to agree upon three people they saw behaving well and they can then report back to the rest of the class. This can be a useful technique for teaching difficult pupils how to behave. First, they get attention and, second, they start to look around the room and focus on good behaviour and see it modelled for them.

Pupils also take note of the way that a teacher dresses. Teachers can model for pupils that they take care of their appearance. Pupils notice details, even down to the colour of nail varnish a teacher wears! This can be a difficult area, because if there is a school uniform in the school, pupils may resent teachers wearing certain items. It is important that pupils are clear that there are rules for teachers too. These may not necessarily be the same as for pupils in terms of the dress code, but nevertheless, there are rules. Some schools insist on men wearing a jacket and tie, for example. The key thing which pupils will be aware of is whether the teacher takes care to wear clothes which are clean and tidy. Sandra always found that wearing different clothes every day and, in particular, bright colours seemed to alter pupils' moods. Role modelling sensible dress also prepares pupils for the world of work where they may have to wear a uniform or certain prescribed clothes.

MODELLING FEELINGS

Teachers need to model for pupils how to express the whole range of feelings appropriately. Feelings are often collapsed into four categories: 'mad' (angry), 'sad', 'glad' and 'bad' (fear). Let us look in more detail at anger. 'Anyone can become angry – that is easy. But to be angry with the right person, to the right degree, at the right time, for the right purpose, and in the right way – that is not easy' (Aristotle, *The Nicomachean Ethics*, quoted in Goleman, 1996).

Anger, while it is often connected with uncomfortable images, such as abuse and violence, is nevertheless a natural emotion which provides us with the physical and emotional energy to help us through situations in which we need protection.

People may disagree about what anger is, as it can mean different things to different people depending on their upbringing and experiences. Some other words for angry include annoyed, resentful, irritable, frustrated and hostile.

Pupils often misbehave in the classroom because they are angry. Their misbehaviour may take the form of being verbally aggressive and swearing or being physically aggressive and violent. Others may express their anger in a different way such as crying. In other words, they display anger in an inappropriate way. Pupils need therefore to be taught anger management.

Anger management involves the following:

- understanding what anger is and how it affects the body
- recognising triggers to anger
- looking at the damaging effects of both passive and aggressive ways of dealing with anger
- safely releasing anger which may have been bottled up
- replacing old patterns of behaviour
- dealing with other people's anger.

Teachers can model appropriate ways of expressing anger (see Assertiveness on p.43-4).

The teacher can ask pupils how they feel when someone is not listening to them. Pupils can offer ideas and feelings about not being listened to and the teacher can then use these ideas as a springboard to explore how a teacher might feel when a class or individual is not listening.

The teacher can model by talking to another pupil how loudly they want the class to speak to each other. Pupils then can hear what is an acceptable noise level. They no longer have to guess what they think is acceptable because it has been modelled for them. If a class is too noisy when they are talking in groups, then the teacher can model the noise level that is acceptable and then the noise the class was making. The teacher can then ask the class which noise level was more acceptable.

The teacher might also give pupils permission to ask them to talk more quietly. Again, the pupils cannot complain when the teacher is setting an example and following the same rules.

Some pupils have an unfortunate way of sounding rude or aggressive even when they do not mean to be. The teacher can show them a less aggressive way of saying what they want without annoying other people. The pupils will begin to realise that by just changing their tone they can sound friendlier and more helpful. The teacher can also demonstrate how a smile might look cheeky and how a sneer can easily be turned into a smile.

WHAT BEHAVIOUR SHOULD WE BE MODELLING?

We want to model behaviour that helps a pupil to be in the 'I'm OK' Life Position. It is also important that we help them develop a positive attitude towards other pupils in the classroom.

We have already discussed what OK behaviour for a teacher might be and the examples of behaviour below are some of the suggestions made by pupils that Sandra worked with.

- firm but fair
- respects pupils
- works hard
- understands and cares
- good sense of humour
- patient and calm
- treats pupils as human beings
- is willing to listen.

Now let us compare how similar or different the OK behaviour of a teacher is to that of OK pupil behaviour.

OK teacher behaviour
- Criticises behaviour not pupil
- Respects pupils and is not biased
These two aspects show how the teacher can model the idea that 'People are OK'.

- Cares
- Is aware of their own rights and those of the pupils
- Is assertive and firm but fair
- Is willing to understand a pupil's problem
- Praises pupils.

Pupils' ideas of OK teacher behaviour
- Respect for themselves and others
- Aware of the needs of pupils

- Understands and cares
- Patient and calm
- Firm but fair
- Is willing to listen
- Encourages, praises and gets on with pupils.

These five aspects demonstrate how the teacher can model how people should relate to each other as in 'I'm OK, You're OK'.

- Shows a willingness to learn
- Works hard   • Works hard
- Everyone does their best   • Knowledgeable about their subject
- Anyone can make mistakes

These four aspects show how the teacher can model that they are interested in learning.

- Believes (and says) that everyone can
  take responsibility for their behaviour.
- Believes and encourages everyone to   • Treats pupils as individuals
  reflect on their behaviour
- Believes and accepts explicitly that   • Treats pupils as human beings
  people can change

These three aspects show how the teacher can model that everyone can think and change

In the left-hand column, OK teacher behaviour, the teacher would be modelling attitudes, feelings and behaviour that show pupils explicitly how they can learn to become independent learners, skilful communicators and caring people who are able if necessary to defend their rights or the rights of other people assertively. By modelling the OK behaviour, the teacher will be helping some pupils to move to the 'I'm OK, you're OK' Life Position.

There will be some qualities in the list that Sandra's pupils came up with that a teacher might not possess. However, by observing other teachers modelling these qualities, a teacher can learn some of them. In other words, teachers too can learn from good modelling, hence observing other good teachers or team teaching when there is an opportunity is important.

The division of OK behaviour in our list is artificial, in reality, all types of OK behaviour are linked and interconnected. However, the division of the OK behaviour into headings is a way of defining the different aspects. It makes it explicitly clear to the teacher the four types of behaviour they need to be modelling:

- That people are OK (Philosophical Assumption 1: People are OK).
- How everyone should relate to other people in the classroom (Life Position: I'm OK, You're OK).
- That they are interested in learning.
- That everyone has the ability to think and change their behaviour (Philosophical Assumption 2: Everyone has the capacity to think and Philosophical Assumption 3: People decide their own destiny and these decisions can be changed).

Notice that the three Philosophical Assumptions of Transactional Analysis can be found within two of these types of behaviour, as indicated above in brackets, as can the most healthy Life Position.

Let us now look at each of these in more detail.

People are OK

Teachers should not be rude, sarcastic or disrespectful to pupils. However, there are classes that will annoy anyone. Think of 9Z:

- They never listen.
- They are rude.
- They write on resources.
- They argue among themselves.

You may well be saying to yourself that no one is a saint, everyone has said something rude or sarcastic to a group like this. Yet 9Z are just the sort of group who need 'I'm OK, you're OK' behaviour modelled for them. It is important that teachers model this Life Position in their classroom and believe that every pupil has the potential to change and behave in an OK way. To do this, the teacher needs to separate the pupil's behaviour from the pupil. The bad behaviour is not OK but the pupil is still intrinsically OK as a person. The teacher needs to believe that the pupil can change and move to the 'I'm OK, you're OK' Life Position in their classroom. However, the pupil will not change unless they are shown a different way of behaving.

Groups like 9Z are made up of individuals who find it difficult to show respect to others because they have little or no respect for themselves. Therefore, the teacher needs to model and teach them ways of developing self-respect and respect for others. This can be modelled and taught using praise. Pupils learn to nurture themselves through positive thoughts and Strokes. They also learn to nurture other pupils. By focusing on the positive things about a pupil, the teacher is helping them to develop their own self-esteem.

How people relate to each other in the classroom: I'm OK, you're OK

A class such as 9Z must also be shown a more positive and effective way of getting their own needs met. Their teacher can model for the class ways of getting what they want through assertive behaviour rather than by using aggressive or manipulative patterns of behaviour.

It seems appropriate here to look in more detail at what we mean by Assertiveness.

Teachers can model appropriate ways of expressing anger by being assertive. Teachers have rights and needs in a classroom. It is essential that they maintain their own 'I'm OK, you're OK' Life Position while they are getting their needs met and do not push classes or individuals into the 'I'm not OK' Life Position. Teachers therefore need to model for their pupils, healthy and respectful ways of getting their own needs and rights met. The 'three-pronged attack' is a useful tool for doing this.

Step 1 Needs/Rights

Assertiveness is about understanding what your needs and rights are as a teacher and expressing or explaining them clearly. You have the right as a teacher to be able to teach. It is important to see this as your right and to value it. No pupil should be allowed to stop you from doing your job. Communicate clearly with pupils by being specific about what you need and the behaviour you would like from pupils in order to get your needs met. 'In this lesson I will need pupils to be quiet for five minutes so I can explain ideas clearly.'

Step 2 Feelings

Explain to a class or individual how you feel about their behaviour. If a pupil talks, tell them how it makes you feel. 'I am disappointed that someone I like is talking and not cooperating with me.' 'I am getting frustrated and angry because you are talking. It's stopping me from teaching.'

Step 3 Consequences

Pupils need to know that if they infringe on your rights, then there will be consequences. Tell pupils calmly, forcefully and clearly what the consequences of their actions will be if they continue to interrupt you. 'I will move you if you interrupt me again.' Here you are teaching pupils where the boundaries, the limit of their behaviour is.

This simple three-step approach can be taught to pupils as a way of resolving conflict effectively. Pupils learn that they have choices. Other pupils cannot wind them up, tease them and make them angry unless they give up their power. They can choose to be assertive and no longer be either a Victim or a Persecutor. It is important that pupils know how to be assertive, in order to avoid them expressing their anger inappropriately.

A useful way of remembering this approach can be found in the sentence:
'**E**ven **F**ish **N**eed **C**onfidence' in which the first letters of each word stand for:

- **E**xplanations
- **F**eelings
- **N**eeds
- **C**onsequences.

(Lindenfield 1992)

Be prepared to say sorry or apologise

While it is important to model for pupils how to be assertive, pupils also need to know what to do if they are wrong. By being prepared to apologise for their own unfair behaviour, the teacher, emphasises that no one in the lesson, including the teacher, is allowed to be unfair.

State your rights and needs as a teacher: 'No one is allowed to be unfair to me. I must be allowed to teach.' Make the pupils aware of their rights: 'If I am unfair or upset you, come and see me and I will apologise to you. However, when you are unfair to me I will expect you to apologise.' You might do this with individual pupils or you may apologise to a whole class for being unfair or not listening properly. You will find that by adopting this approach pupils will not be as defensive about themselves. They will be prepared to admit they are wrong. By doing this, you are modelling how to move from 'I'm not OK, you're OK' to 'I'm OK, you're OK'.

It is worth noting that some pupils will come from home backgrounds where being wrong is dangerous and admitting you are wrong might end up in violence. Therefore, they are prepared for you to say sorry but they will not. By apologising for their own poor behaviour, a teacher models for the pupils that everyone including the teacher can change their behaviour. The teacher is also modelling for the pupils how they can move from 'I'm not OK and other people are not OK' to 'I'm OK and everyone in the classroom is OK'. Pupils learn that Life Positions, moods and attitudes can and should be changed when people are behaving unfairly.

Aim to create a safe classroom environment by nurturing pupils. Do not allow other pupils to be rude to each other. Tell them: 'No one in this room is allowed to be rude to other people including me.'

Learn pupils' names and learn them fast. Knowing a pupil's name is important. Think about how you feel when someone gets your name wrong. Therefore, get the pupil's name right. Check with the pupil the pronunciation and if they want it shortened. Sometimes it is, however, inappropriate to use pupils' nicknames!

Greet pupils as they come into your room with a smile and a positive comment: 'It's nice to see you', 'Did you have a good weekend?'

Tell classes or individuals what you like about their behaviour. An assertive person takes and gives praise naturally. Pupils need to be taught how to take and give praise. Find out from other staff anything they have done well. When you see pupils individually around school you can tell them, for example; 'Mrs Robins is really impressed with the work you have produced in her art lessons. Your work is on display, I'll go up to the art room and look at it.'

We can demonstrate to pupils that they matter by giving them our time and attention. It is important that we model good listening for pupils to copy. Don't turn your back on pupils or walk away from them as they are talking. Also don't do another job or concentrate on something else while they are talking to you. If you do not listen properly be prepared to apologise. Check with pupils that you have heard them properly: 'John, can I check with you that I heard you correctly. I think you said … am I correct?'

Teach pupils good listening skills by getting them to talk to the person next to them. Give each person two minutes to talk on a subject without interruption; the person listening has to then tell the other person what they have heard. The person who was being listened to gives feedback on how good the listener was and the things they did that helped them to talk – eye contact, nodding of head, etc. They can also talk about the things that put them off talking such as tapping their fingers, playing with a pen or no eye contact.

The teacher can teach listening skills by giving pupils a number of things to write and draw on a page. The teacher puts the correct version on the OHT and pupils swap and mark each other's books.

The teacher can make a pupil chairperson and emphasise that only pupils with their hands up can speak. The teacher is then forced to put their hand up in order to be listened to.

Humour is a spontaneous quality and therefore it is difficult to learn. However, if you can use it, a simple but golden rule is never to use sarcasm. Humour should make pupils feel OK and still valued. It should not be used to make you feel OK while they feel not OK. Therefore, as teachers we should laugh with pupils and not at them. You can also direct humour at yourself and send yourself up. This shows pupils that you are human.

Do not promise pupils anything unless you are going to keep your word. Model reliability by being on time, meeting deadlines and marking their work. In your classroom make sure pupils know that they will always be treated fairly and respectfully. If an opportunity comes up to help a pupil, take it. Make pupils aware that if they have a problem, you are willing to listen to them and offer them help.

In terms of relating to other people too, the teacher needs to make sure that pupils understand that OK behaviour means that no sexism, racism or violence will be tolerated in the classroom.

The teacher is interested in learning

If teachers want pupils to be enthusiastic, energetic and diligent workers, then they need to model this behaviour for their pupils by being organised, teaching to the best of their ability and marking their books regularly. We as teachers must keep to deadlines if we want pupils to do the same.

It is important too that teachers are enthusiastic about their subject. Visualise the class, as you want them to be. Concentrate on the positive things in the classroom, rather than negatives. Aim to sound enthusiastic even if you do not always feel in the mood. You will find if you act as if you are enjoying yourself, pretty soon you will actually feel good about the class and the work. This positive attitude will filter down and pupils will start to realise that being positive about things is the norm in your lesson. Energy creates more energy and enthusiasm is infectious.

By arriving at our lessons on time with a sense of purpose, pupils soon get the message that this is a subject that matters. Writing the lesson outcomes on the board will also give the pupils a sense of purpose. At the end of the lesson the teacher can ask them to write down three big ideas they have learnt. The pupils are gaining an understanding that in your lesson you expect them to know something at the end of the lesson. This technique makes them accountable for their own learning.

With a difficult class the teacher might choose a pupil to be the teacher and ask the pupil to judge whether the behaviour they are about to model helps pupils to keep on task and do their best. The teacher then models the bad behaviour that is preventing the class from being on task, such as playing with equipment, talking loudly, etc. The teacher might then ask the class to come up with three ways of behaving that would help pupils to learn more. The teacher or members of the class could model the new behaviour and explain why it is better.

Involving pupils in the learning process emphasises that the teacher thinks that they are OK. This may involve asking the pupils for their opinion about which work they have enjoyed or areas of work that might need modifying. The teacher is teaching the pupils to be reflective by modelling reflective thinking themselves. Sandra developed, as part of the RAISE project, a lesson feedback form, where pupils had an opportunity to give their opinions about each part of the lesson on a scale of 1–10. There were also questions about their own attitude in the lesson, such as:

- How hard did you work?
- How good was your behaviour?
- What helped you to learn?
- What helped you to behave?

There may also be occasions when you want to give pupils a minute or two to think about something in silence. Get pupils to listen to what 'quiet' is, so they know what absolute silence means both for the teacher and for the pupils.

Have pupils write their own work targets or behaviour targets at the start of the lesson and then reward them for meeting the targets. At the end of the lesson they can write in their book: 'Mr Jenkins was pleased today because I completed all my work.' The teacher might start a new lesson by asking the class to write down something they have learnt and something positive they did that helped them to learn.

Getting pupils to write targets can help pupils to address Driver behaviour (see Life Scripts) such as 'Hurry Up' pupils who rush through work and make careless mistakes. Modelling meeting deadlines can help pupils with 'Try Hard' Drivers, who are very enthusiastic at the start of a project but never finish it. Model and share with pupils examples of good working habits, good work or good behaviour. Show them examples of good work.

Have pupils mark each other's work. First, develop the marking scheme with them. Talk about the types of comments that are useful and sensitive to write on another pupil's work. Give them examples of comments (good or bad). Which comments do they think are most useful? Marking another pupil's work gives them a chance to think about what makes a good piece of work. It also helps them to develop sensitivity towards other pupils. It allows the whole class to develop a class view of what constitutes good work. Finally, the whole class can celebrate success together. It helps them form an identity of a class that works hard, does its best and produces quality work. The teacher also has an opportunity to teach the class how to give and receive praise.

There are lots of variations on getting pupils to mark their own work. The teacher can put up an OHT with different levels and pupils decide which level best describes their work or the work of someone else. Or the teacher can model independent and quiet working habits by doing the same work as the class. For example, with a class that finds it difficult to settle and work quietly, the teacher can give the class a time limit and do the same piece of work. If the teacher is asking for quiet from the class, it is because, as a good learner, they need quiet in order to complete the work. This sends out a message to the class that the work is important and even the best worker in the class needs quiet. It gives the class the opportunity to see a good learner in action.

We can model that everyone makes mistakes and everyone is fallible including the teacher. We do not have to be perfect all the time. Learning involves risk taking. Making mistakes is OK. Tell pupils that it is OK to be wrong as long as you do your best and you learn how not to make that mistake again. It is not OK for them to be sloppy or not bothered about their work.

People can think and change

When pupils make mistakes, we need to teach them that they have options. They need to be taught how to solve problems, by thinking them through and not sink into feelings such as anger or sadness when they make mistakes. Therefore, it is important that the teacher models a positive approach to problems and shows that they can be overcome.

Pupils need to learn to take responsibility for their own behaviour. They have to be taught that their behaviour has consequences and they need to make the right choices, by thinking about them.

Another extremely important technique in thinking about and changing behaviour is 'reframing' behaviour. This is an important form of modelling. If you are trying to get a pupil to change their behaviour, you need to substitute it with the correct behaviour. Some of them may not have had this modelled for them at home and thus need to be taught. After all, it is our job to educate the pupils in every respect.

Pupil: Shift, Jason, I can't see the board your big fat head is in the way.

Teacher: Let's do that differently, Lee. What is another way of saying, 'shift'? How about trying 'excuse me'? Secondly, it's not very nice to say someone has a 'big fat head'; how about 'Could you please move your head because I can't see?'

Pupil: 'Excuse me, Jason, could you move your head because I can't see?'

Teacher: Now look at the difference in Jason's reaction

Pupil: Yes, he moved straight away!

In this chapter, we have discussed how modelling is an effective way of showing and teaching pupils to adopt an 'I'm OK, you're OK' Life Position and of demonstrating the three philosophical assumptions of Transactional Analysis.

Chapter 9

Ego States

… a consistent pattern of feeling and experience directly related to a corresponding consistent pattern of behaviour.

(Berne, quoted in Stewart and Joines, 1991)

… a system of feelings accompanied by a related set of behaviour patterns.

(Berne, 1984)

ACTIVITY

Think of a pupil that you always tend to argue with. What do they do that annoys you? How do you react? Do you always react and speak to them in the same way? What is the tone of your voice like?

There are some classes or individuals that as teachers we fail to connect with. It is as if both the pupil and the teacher get locked into a set way of relating and communicating with each other. This lack of communication can result in:

- misunderstanding
- bad feelings
- arguments
- indifference.

It is often difficult for a teacher to pinpoint exactly why this failure in communication happens. In this chapter we are going to investigate what Ego States are and how they can be used by teachers to improve their communication skills so that they can avoid getting involved in conflict or they can stop it escalating once it has started.

ACTIVITY

Look at the way the teachers below react to the same incident. What do you notice about their behaviour?

The pupil has defaced the teacher's work.

> Teacher 1: You have just started World War II, sonny. You can do lots more colouring in during detention. That should wipe the smile off your face.

> Teacher 2: I am not happy with what you have done. I will see you at the end of the lesson about this. If you misbehave again you will leave the room.

> Teacher 3: I spent hours doing these sheets. You have ruined them. It's not fair. I'm not going give you any more of my sheets. I feel like scribbling all over your magazine to see how it makes you feel.

Each of these teachers has reacted differently. The teachers are operating from different Ego States. The first teacher was in Parent Ego State, the second teacher was in Adult and the third teacher was in Child. (Note that when we are referring to the Ego States, we use a capital letter for Parent, Adult and Child.)

STRUCTURAL EGO STATE MODEL

The structural model describes the content of each Ego State. It is known as structural because it is about the structure of a person's psychology. If we analyse a person's personality in terms of ego states, we use 'structural analysis'. According to Stewart and Joines (1991), there are three ego states in the structural model: Parent – 'behaviour, thoughts and feelings copied from parents or parent figures'; Adult –

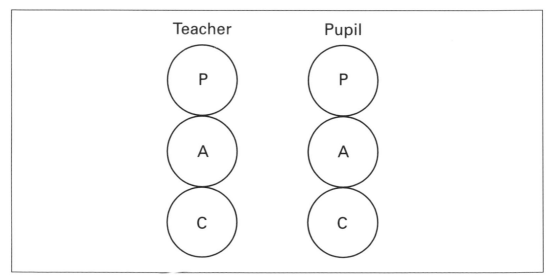

Figure 9.1   Ego States: structural model
Note: The three-circle logo is a registered trademark of the International Transactional Analysis Association and is reproduced here with permission.

'behaviours, thoughts and feelings which are a direct response to the here and now' (testing reality); Child – 'behaviours, thoughts and feelings replayed from childhood' (see Figure 9.1). Figure 9.1 shows the three Ego States in TA; P=Parent, A=Adult and C=Child.

FUNCTIONAL EGO STATE MODEL

This is about the way a person behaves or functions in the world. The three Ego States are further subdivided.

The Parent Ego State is subdivided into two parts:

• Controlling Parent (how to control/discipline others).
• Nurturing Parent (how to look after others).

The Adult is not subdivided. Any behaviour which responds to here and now reality using all the person's grown up resources is in Adult.

The Child is also subdivided:

• Free Child (spontaneous and natural).
• Adapted Child (adapting behaviour to gain approval).

See Figure 9.2.

So how do we use these in the classroom? Transactional Analysis identifies a number of Ego States that a teacher may be in or choose to be in.

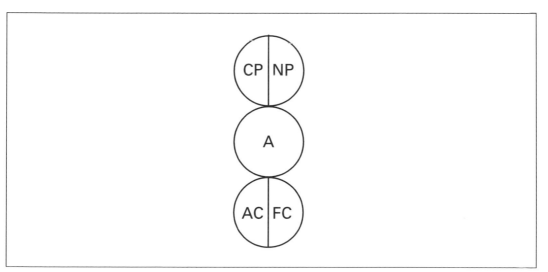

Figure 9.2 Ego States: functional model
The functional model of Ego States subdivides the Parent into Controlling or Critical Parent (CP) and Nurturing Parent (NP). It also divides the Child Ego State into Adapted Child (AC) and Free Child (FC). The three-circle logo is a registered trademark of the International Transactional Analysis Association and is reproduced here with permission.

- *Controlling Parent: Positive Controlling Parent* This involves the teacher setting sensible rules and making clear to the pupils what is acceptable behaviour.
- *Negative Controlling Parent* The teacher is always nagging, picking fault and criticising. The teacher is persecuting and bullying.
- *Nurturing Parent: Positive Nurturing Parent* The teacher shows care and concern for their pupils, for example, they notice changes in behaviour that may be to do with bullying or pressures in or outside of school.
- *Negative Nurturing Parent* The teacher is in 'I'm OK you're not OK'. They do too much for the pupil and make them weak and not OK.
- *Adult* In this Ego State, the teacher responds to the here and now. This Ego State is useful for problem-solving. The teacher chooses the appropriate Ego State from which to respond to the pupil's behaviour. If, however, a teacher is too much in this Ego State, they can seem cold and machine-like.
- *Adapted Child: Positive Adapted Child* Adapted Child allows us to fit into the family or culture we find ourselves in. When the teacher operates from this Ego State, they will talk politely and show courtesy.
- *Negative Adapted Child* We adapt too readily to what we think other people want us to be and we are not being ourselves, for example, in school a teacher may agree to do something just to please others and then feel resentful later.
- *Free Child: Positive Free Child* We behave in a friendly and creative way. The teacher may go on a trip with pupils and enjoy joining in activities with the pupils, such as going on the rides at an amusement park. Pupils will see a different side to the teacher, one in which the teacher laughs and has fun.
- *Negative Free Child* The teacher behaves in a childish way that is inappropriate; for example, they tell pupils jokes that are inappropriate or swear.

ACTIVITY

Jack Dusay devised the Egogram. This is a way of intuitively deciding how much time you spend in each of the Ego States. (Note that this is the name when you conduct the exercises on other people. If it is carried out on oneself, it is referred to as the 'Psychogram'). See Figure 9.3.

The Egogram is a way of showing how often you use each of the functional Ego States. In this particular case, the idea is to represent what you do in the classroom. The idea is to draw a vertical bar above each Ego State label. The highest of the bars represents how much you use that state.

In Figure 9.3 this teacher would probably set firm boundaries (CP), be quite nurturing (NP) and give pupils some ownership of the learning process through open communication (A) but not have a lot of fun (FC) in the classroom.

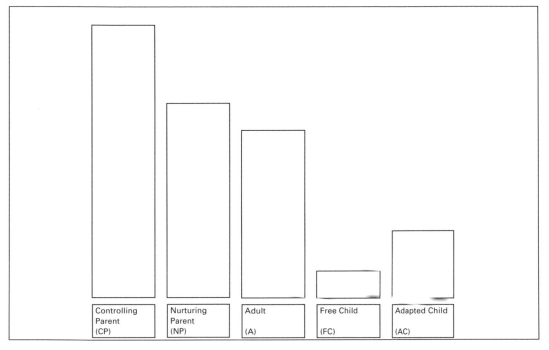

Figure 9.3 Example of an Egogram
Note: The Egogram was developed by Dr John M. Dusay and first published in 'Egograms and the Constancy Hypothesis', *Transactional Analysis Journal*, 2 (3), pp. 37-41. It is reprinted here with the permission of Dr Dusay and the International Transactional Anaylsis Association.

Controlling Parent (CP)	Nurturing Parent (NP)	Adult (A)	Free Child (FC)	Adapted Child (AC)

Figure 9.4 Your own Egogram

Let us look at these Ego States in the context of the classroom. Draw your own Egogram and draw bar graphs to show how much time you spend in each of the Ego States during a day in school. (See Figure 9.4.)

Obviously with different groups your Egogram could be different. You may have found that you spend too much time in one Ego State.

- Do you need to have more or less Controlling Parent in your lessons?
- Do you need more humour in your lessons? (Free Child)
- Do you need to be in the Adult Ego State more?
- Do you need to nurture yourself or the pupils more?

ACTIVITY

Consider the problems below and think which of the Ego States would be best for a teacher to be in. Think of things the teacher might say or do in the Ego State you have chosen. Get a pen and paper and jot down the Ego States that might best be used in order to sort these problems out and the things you might say.

Example 1
Robert never shuts up about football and always wants to engage the teacher in talking about football instead of doing his work.

Example 2
Jane is always looking for an argument. She often behaves unfairly but when confronted about her behaviour uses it as an opportunity to blow up and blames teachers for everything being wrong. She often complains at the start of the lesson about you, the teacher or something else.

Example 3
Brian is never on task and is always disturbing other students by touching their equipment.

Example 4
Carol talks when the teacher is talking and then says rude things under her breath.

Here are some suggestions of Ego States (roles) you might choose. You may disagree with the choices and have better ideas. The main thing is that you are being creative and looking to find different ways of managing behaviour and maintaining good relationships.

Example 1

- 'Robert, one more word about football and it's a yellow card.' Here the teacher is in Free Child.
- 'Robert, I know you like football and so do I but we need to get on with the lesson. We can talk about the football at the end of the lesson.' Here the teacher is in Nurturing Parent/Adult.
- 'Robert, you need to get on with your work, I expect you to do well in this subject. I need this work completed by you and it must be completed by the end of the lesson.' The teacher is in Controlling Parent.

Boys like Robert are usually friendly boys who do not get down to work but who respond to humour and friendliness. However, even Robert might need to know where the boundaries of your patience are.

Example 2

- 'You don't sound like you have had a very nice day, Jane. If there is a problem in the lesson, I will help you out. We have to get on with learning.' (Nurturing Parent)
- 'You worked well last lesson, Jane. Let me get started with the lesson and then if there is a problem we can sort it out together.' (Adult)
- 'OK, Jane if there is a problem I know you can sort it out maturely. We need to start the lesson.' (Adult)

The point is that Jane is looking for trouble, so don't give her any opportunity to be a nuisance.

Example 3

- 'Brian, I just want a yes or no answer to this question, would it be fair for me to pick your pen up and throw it around the room?' (Controlling Parent/Adult)
- 'Brian, if you touch anyone else's equipment, you will be moved to sit at my desk.' (Controlling Parent)

Brian is the type of boy who needs clear signals about what will happen. However, you might want to add a nurturing comment, such as, 'Brian you are a pleasant boy, don't spoil all your good work with silly behaviour. If you need equipment I am willing to lend things to pleasant pupils.'

Example 4

- 'Carol, you listened well last lesson, everyone else is quiet and they are waiting to be taught. I am going to get on with the lesson.' (Controlling Parent/Adult)
- 'Carol, is there a problem? If so, you can talk about it once I have finished talking to the rest of the group.' (Nurturing Parent/Adult)

- 'I need everyone in the class to be quiet. I need this so I can teach a good lesson. Is there anyone who does not understand why I need this?' (Adult)
- 'Carol, no one is allowed to stop me teaching. You have a choice; stop talking or I will move you to sit on your own.' (Controlling Parent)

With pupils like Carol and Jane you need to judge what type of strategy is going to work from lesson to lesson. They are angry pupils, so anger is generally going to make them angrier. Using a friendly, nurturing tone will give them little to fight back against.

It is worth pointing out that with individuals or groups who are particularly difficult, it may be necessary to start off in Controlling Parent. This may involve, for example, assertively setting firm boundaries in order to get the behaviour you want. It is only then that you can go on to use the other Ego States. This is because the pupils may have had erratic parenting which has left them confused about how to behave and respond and they therefore have little or no access to their Adult Ego State. This needs to be modelled for them.

It is useful to experiment with Ego States. Brainstorm the types of behaviour pupils might exhibit in the classroom. Think about which Ego State would be best to use and then say out loud what you might say when in this Ego State. What does your voice sound like? Does it match the Ego State you think you are using? It might be useful to use a tape recorder so that you can hear your own voice. Sometimes we can think we are operating from Nurturing Parent but our voices sound as if we are in Adult or Controlling Parent.

The way teachers use their voice can convey meaning to the pupil without the teacher having to explain fully what they mean. For example, David kept a boy behind to talk about his lack of coursework. That lesson the boy had produced some coursework and wanted to take it home to show his mother. David told him he could take his coursework home but he would be responsible for it. A cleaner was in the room at the time and after the boy had left she commented on the way David's voice had changed. She said, 'He won't lose that work. You could tell from your voice that there would be trouble if it went missing.' David had changed Ego States without knowing it. He had moved from Adult to Controlling Parent.

There are occasions when, as teachers, we say something and we are unaware of the message our voice is sending out. We may mean to be nurturing but our voice may sound hard and harsh. There are times when pupils show us work and our voice may sound tired and bored. It is therefore useful to think 'Is my voice matching the Ego State I want to be operating from?'

Often we get locked into transactions with pupils that are unhelpful and negative. We routinely talk to a class or an individual in a set way. In conflict, the teacher may forget that they have options – different Ego States. For example:

James: I hate this lesson. (Rebellious Child/Free Child)

Teacher: Shut up and get on with your work. (Controlling Parent)

This approach by the teacher is likely to fuel James's anger and anti-social behaviour. James may go on to say, 'Why don't you shut up?' or something else that fuels confrontation.

Here is another approach. The teacher chooses a different Ego State to respond from.

James: I hate this lesson.

Teacher: I'm sorry to hear that. You have good ideas when you try. What are you finding difficult?

The teacher has responded from Nurturing Parent and it is much more difficult for James to continue to be aggressive. We can encourage pupils to discover and use different Ego States by reframing their behaviour.

A pupil may say, 'Give me that.' This can be reframed by the teacher modelling the behaviour they want. For example, the teacher can say to the pupil. 'Try saying: "Please, Mrs Brown, may I have a pencil?"' and then ask the pupil 'Which one of these is most likely to make me smile and give you a pencil?'

Using different Ego States can help teachers to become more skilful communicators. They give teachers a choice. No longer does the teacher respond in an automatic and possibly ineffective and confrontational way, but acts instead with awareness. The teacher can tailor their response to a particular pupil or situation and can consciously decide which Ego States best meet the needs of that pupil, situation or group.

In other words, when teachers are aware of which Ego State they are using and can readily access the other two Ego States by monitoring what they say and how they say it, they can avoid, defuse or resolve conflict more easily.

Chapter 10

Transactions

An exchange of strokes constitutes a transaction, *which is the unit of social discourse.*

(Berne, 1984)

Since the theory is called Transactional Analysis, it makes sense to say that part of the theory is about analysing transactions! Communication is at the heart of good teaching. Teachers need to be able to communicate their ideas about their subject in a fresh, relevant, stimulating and authoritative manner. They need to communicate to pupils what they are doing well and how they can improve. Teachers also need to communicate clearly, sensitively and fairly what they do not like about a pupil's behaviour. However, communication is not a one-way process. If pupils do not either want to listen or communicate, then pretty soon it can feel like teachers are talking to themselves.

In the last chapter we investigated how teachers can skilfully use Ego States in order to avoid conflict and maintain communication between them and the pupil. In Transactional Analysis, this type of communication is called a Transaction. In this chapter we aim to explore Transactions in more detail.

There are three ways that people can communicate. They can use

- a Complementary Transaction
- a Crossed Transaction
- an Ulterior Transaction.

COMPLEMENTARY TRANSACTIONS

Pupil: I'm really sorry, miss. I haven't done my homework. I've got a letter from my mum. We had problems last night, my brother had to go to hospital.

Teacher: Thanks for explaining. It's not a problem. Let's arrange another time for you to complete the homework.

The pupil from their Adult Ego State addresses the teacher's Adult Ego State. The teacher responds from their Adult Ego State. The transactional vectors are parallel. This is a Complementary Transaction. In this type of transaction the pupil had expectations about how they would be responded to. See Figure 10.1.

Berne (1984) stated that: 'Communication will proceed smoothly as long as transactions are complementary.' So it seems likely in this example that the teacher and pupil will be able to continue their conversation because they are fulfilling the requirements of a Complementary Transaction. They will sort out the missing homework.

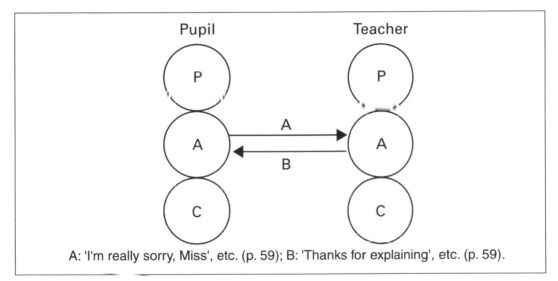

A: 'I'm really sorry, Miss', etc. (p. 59); B: 'Thanks for explaining', etc. (p. 59).

Figure 10.1 A Complementary Transaction representing an Adult to Adult transaction
Note: The three-circle logo is registered trademark of the International Transactional Analysis Association and is reproduced here with permission.

CROSSED TRANSACTION

Now let us look at the same transaction but this time the teacher will respond to the pupil with a Crossed Transaction.

Pupil: I'm really sorry, Miss. I haven't done my homework I've got a letter from my mum. We had problems last night, my brother had to go to hospital.

Teacher: I'm not interested in excuses. You know the rules. No homework equals detention.

As in the first example the pupil from their Adult Ego State has tried to access the teacher's Adult, however, this time the teacher has responded from their Controlling

Parent Ego State. See Figure 10.2. 'When a transaction is crossed, a break in communication results and one or both individuals will need to shift ego states in order for communication to be re-established' (Berne, quoted in Stewart and Joines, 1991).

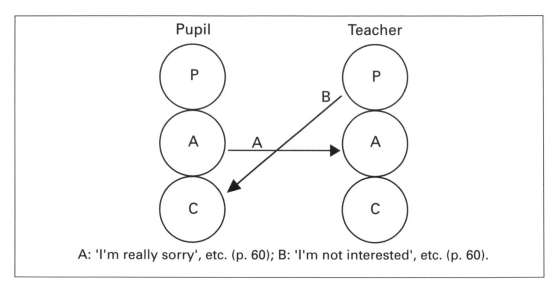

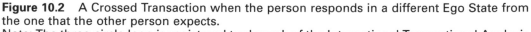

A: 'I'm really sorry', etc. (p. 60); B: 'I'm not interested', etc. (p. 60).

Figure 10.2   A Crossed Transaction when the person responds in a different Ego State from the one that the other person expects.
Note: The three-circle logo is registered trademark of the International Transactional Analysis Association and is reproduced here with permission.

The pupil might react in a shocked, surprised or hurt way. The pupil may move from Adult to Rebellious Child. This change of Ego States will only encourage the teacher to become entrenched in Negative Controlling Parent behaviour.

Many pupils will find it difficult to change to more positive Ego States. Once in Rebellious Child, they need to be encouraged out of that Ego State. However, when some pupils get irritable or angry they will begin to get lost in their own internal world (see Chapters 16 and 17, Scripts and Games). The teacher may find themselves getting sucked into irrational arguments and Games.

In the previous chapter on Ego States, we saw that a teacher can maintain communication by choosing a different Ego State. The Rebellious Child wants the teacher to be in Controlling Parent. It gives them something to fight against, something to fuel their feelings of anger and possible injustice. However, the teacher who says: 'You sound angry, have you had a horrible day?' is able to maintain communication because they have responded from their Positive Nurturing Parent Ego State rather than their Negative Controlling Parent Ego State. The pupil may then move from Rebellious Child to Adapted Child because they feel they are being listened to and there is a chance that they might be treated fairly.

Teacher (very loudly): Don't do that!

Pupil: I wasn't doing anything.

The teacher realises that they have made a mistake and then moves from Controlling Parent into Adult.

Teacher: Ian, it was unfair of me to shout at you. I am sorry, but I don't want you to behave like that because it is disruptive.

Pupil sulks but grudgingly says 'OK.' In this example the teacher has changed Ego States and has stopped operating from Controlling Parent and begun to operate from Adult. This has encouraged the pupil to move from Rebellious Child to Adult and accept the teacher's apology.

In a classroom, there will be occasions when a teacher crosses a pupil's transaction. For example:

Pupil: Do you think Manchester United will win the league?

Teacher: I am not going to discuss that now. Get on with your work.

Pupils are more willing to accept a Crossed Transaction when they have an overview of the lesson. If they feel the Crossed Transaction was unfair, they know that at the end of the lesson they can see the teacher and they will be treated fairly because they know that the teacher models fairness in their lesson.

As teachers we need to be aware of the price that we pay for Crossed Transactions. If a pupil has stopped listening to us, all the shouting in the world is not going to change their behaviour. However, there are things that as teachers we cannot and must not accept in our lesson and that will always cause Crossed Transactions:

- a pupil stopping the teacher from teaching
- a pupil being violent
- a pupil bullying other pupils
- a pupil being racist or sexist towards other pupils
- pupil damaging resources or other pupil's property.

ULTERIOR TRANSACTIONS

Pupil: I don't understand what you saying.

Teacher: What exactly don't you understand?

Pupil: Everything. Mrs Bruce explained things much better last year.

The pupil's transaction is an Ulterior Transaction. The open social message is that Mrs Bruce explained things clearly. The covert psychological message is that the teacher is not as good as Mrs Bruce. See Figure 10.3. In figure 10.3 the dotted lines represent the ulterior (hidden) message. This type of transaction allows the pupil to have a dig at the teacher. It can wind the teacher up without them really understanding why. The reason for this is that the pupil has a hidden agenda. They want the teacher to feel bad (see Chapter 17, Games). The pupil sounds as if they are accessing their Adult Ego State. They are giving their opinion, however, the psychological message is coming from the pupil's Negative Controlling Parent.

The best way of dealing with Ulterior Transactions is by operating in the Adult Ego State and analysing what is happening. The teacher can only have a relationship with this pupil by confronting the ulterior message in a calm, assertive and adult manner.

Teacher: William, you seemed to be saying to me that Mrs Bruce explained things more clearly to you.

William: I never said that.

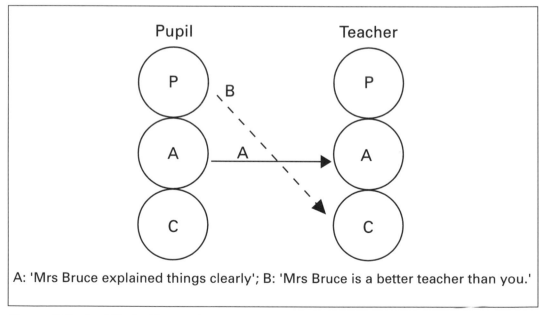

A: 'Mrs Bruce explained things clearly'; B: 'Mrs Bruce is a better teacher than you.'

Figure 10.3   An Ulterior Transaction
Note: The three-circle logo is a registered trademark of the International Transactional Analysis Association and is reproduced here with permission

Teacher: You may not have said that but that's what I heard. What things did Mrs Bruce do last year that helped you?

William: We never went so fast through the work.

Teacher: OK. I will think about what you have said and check out with other pupils without mentioning your name whether they feel the pace of the lesson is too fast. I will talk to you again next lesson.

The teacher has managed to turn this situation into a learning opportunity and can check whether what William has said is true. They also confront William in a fair manner and stop his Game (see Chapter 17). William has been shown that he can get his needs met by being more honest with his teacher. There is now an opportunity for communication between the two of them.

'Sir, Jenny threw my pen on the floor.' April has thrown her own pen on the floor. Here the pupil on a social level is operating in Parent while psychologically they are operating in Rebellious Child. When the whole class know that the teacher consistently models fair behaviour, this type of behaviour is generally a non-starter, both with the teacher and the class.

By maintaining Adult awareness in the classroom the teacher can choose the most appropriate Ego State from which to respond to the pupil. This allows the teacher to keep Transactions complementary if they choose to. The teacher's responses will have a consistency, a sense of fairness about them. Pupils will find they are less surprised in their Transactions with the teacher. There is no doubt that pupils like teachers to be predictable in their behaviour patterns. It makes them feel insecure if a teacher is 'moody' and responds differently each day. Also, by maintaining communication with the pupil there is a chance that their behaviour can be modified or changed.

Communication between teacher and the pupils is more likely to remain complementary when many of the ideas explored in this book are put into practice. Through modelling the behaviour the teacher wants, the teacher is encouraging the pupils to respond to them from their own Adult Ego State. When pupils know through Contracts, shared outcomes and rewards what to expect, there is less need for them to find out where the teacher's boundaries are or to get involved in Transactions that are crossed. They know the lesson is about achieving things and gaining recognition from the teacher through praise and rewards. Therefore the need to use Crossed Transactions or Ulterior Transactions to gain recognition disappears.

Chapter 11
Relationships

Accepting yourself makes it easier to accept the blemishes and failures of others without judgements and condemnation.

(Samways, 1997)

It is an interesting idea to consider that the relationships we have with others often reflect the relationships we have with ourselves: the interpersonal mirrors the intrapersonal. If you do not feel OK about yourself, it will therefore be difficult for pupils to feel OK in your classroom. This can mean, for example, that teachers who shout, are aggressive or sarcastic often do not have much self-esteem. It is as if they 'take it out' on the pupils. On the other hand, teachers who are confident tend to be calm, nurturing and fair.

Activity

Write down the ingredients that help to make good relationships between teachers and their pupils.

Relationships in the classroom, as in the rest of our lives, are vital to success. Ask any pupil why they enjoy a subject and they will often say that they like the teacher. It is difficult to learn anything from someone whom you dislike or do not respect. Good relationships between a teacher and their class sometimes have an indefinable and magical feel about them. As a teacher, we cannot always explain why we have a warm relationship with some classes and yet cold, more distant relationships with others. However, by analysing the qualities that make up a good, OK relationship with some of our classes, we can learn to consciously develop these qualities with more of our classes.

WHAT DO TEACHERS AND PUPILS WANT FROM THEIR RELATIONSHIPS?

- politeness and civility
- respect
- feeling appreciated and valued

- pupils doing their best
- fairness
- pupils are aware of the consequences of their bad behaviour (They do not always agree with the teacher but they are able to empathise with the teacher.)
- sense of humour and fun (The class laughs with the teacher, not at them.)
- reliability and trust
- safety (No one is going to be violent.)
- friendliness (Pupils don't hold grudges. They are on your side.)
- forgiveness (The class accepts that teachers are not always perfect.)

We have already pointed out in Chapter 8, that pupils will want from a teacher the same type of OK behaviour that a teacher will want from them. However, pupils have the right to demand these extra things from a teacher:

- competence (Teachers should be knowledgeable about their subject and proficient in teaching it.)
- adult behaviour
- safety (No one is going to be humiliated or made fun of by the teacher.)

As we have shown earlier, as teachers we cannot demand any behaviour that we do not model and explain to the pupils. We have to set the standard of behaviour that we want in our own classroom. It is important that we as the teacher are organised, interested and enthusiastic about what we are teaching and that we meet deadlines. We have to do our best.

Most of the time as teachers we are operating in our Adult or Parent Ego states. Even when we are in Controlling Parent we can make sure that we are behaving assertively and not aggressively. Pupils will feel valued and involved in rule making if the teacher develops a Contract with them. They will feel safe because they know what to expect from their teacher and they are clear about their role in the classroom. It is important that you respect the pupils' rights and needs as learners but it is equally important that the pupils learn to respect your rights and needs as a teacher.

A model we can use for developing good relationships can be found in the three Philosophical Assumptions of TA:

- People are OK.
- People can think.
- People can change.

PUPILS ARE OK

Pupils will pick up whether their teacher thinks they are OK or not very quickly, so make sure you quickly get to know a pupil's name. Smile at pupils. This shows them that you think they are OK. Be positive about them. Use words like 'mature', 'well behaved', 'clever', 'pleasant', etc. to describe a pupil or class. Be polite to them. Never humiliate or make fun of pupils or use sarcasm. This is often the thing that pupils most dislike about teachers.

Greet pupils as they come through your door. The best Ego State for the teacher to choose to do this in is Positive Nurturing Parent. They can ask pupils if they have had a nice day or ask them if they saw the football last night on television. If it is at the end of the week they might ask pupils if they are doing anything nice over the weekend. This helps the teacher to attach to the pupil. It is much more difficult for the pupils to misbehave if they have made some sort of attachment to their teacher. Attachment can be made throughout the day. Taking the time to say 'hello' to pupils in corridors helps to create attachment between you and them. Whenever you are told something good about a pupil, store it up and tell the pupil in order to reinforce the idea that they are OK.

When we discipline a pupil we must always respect that they as individuals are OK. We dislike the behaviour, not the pupil. Never dislike a pupil. They will sense that you dislike them through body language and it will be difficult for them to have any attachment to you. Therefore always concentrate on something that is good about them. Show that you believe that pupils can change. Just because a pupil has misbehaved once, it does not necessarily mean that they will continue to do it every lesson.

One way we can see pupils as being OK is by seeing things from their viewpoint. Sometimes as teachers we forget what it was like to be teenagers. We forget that things that seem mundane to us are important to the pupils we teach. Falling out with their friends or boyfriend/girlfriend can seem like the end of the world to pupils. Knowing about the 1832 Reform Act, global warming or the dative case in German might be important to us as teachers, but for some pupils it will have little relevance. It is important to show pupils that you can empathise with them and see things from their point of view even when you disagree with them.

Pupils can be valued by the teacher for their individuality. Teachers can show pupils that they are allowed to have feelings and they can be angry with the teacher and other people but they must act in an assertive and not aggressive way. Pupils need to know that they can put forward their view and that you as a teacher will listen to them and act to put right any injustice when you can.

If we want pupils to develop into OK pupils who want to learn and behave, then we as teachers need to model OK behaviour. Make sure that you are always fair and respectful to pupils. By doing this, the teacher in turn can demand respect from the pupils. Make sure that in your classroom you are assertive towards pupils and not aggressive. Model assertive behaviour and use it to make sure that the pupils treat you fairly. Be enthusiastic about your own subject and the work that the pupils produce.

We can show pupils that they matter by giving them time. Make sure that you listen to pupils, however busy you are. Check with pupils that you have understood what they have told you.

PEOPLE CAN THINK AND CHANGE

A healthy relationship is not static, it is something that is constantly changing and evolving. It gives the people involved in the relationship the opportunity to grow and develop their potential. Teachers in a classroom need to promote this type of relationship. The pupils that they teach need to know that their teacher believes in them, and values them. Some pupils will have given up on themselves and see themselves as not OK – stupid, thick, no good at anything, failures. By using Strokes we can help them to see that we value them as both learners and individuals and we can help them to value themselves.

If teachers are to help pupils to become autonomous people, it is essential that they do not rescue pupils. The teacher needs to make the pupil aware of their own personal power and their own resources that solve problems.

We have already seen that developing Contracts with pupils demonstrates to them that their teachers do respect and trust them to be OK, responsible, and capable of overcoming the problems that they might face. Make pupils aware that if they have problems, they can come to you for help. However, as teachers we need to be aware of what type of help we can give and when we can keep confidentiality. Do not rescue pupils but teach them how to solve their own problems. Give them options and make them aware of the types of things you may have to report to other people.

As teachers we can model awareness. We can think about which is the best way to react to pupils. If teachers experiment with the ideas that we have investigated they can change their relationships both with classes and individuals. Being in Adult all the time can give an impression that the teacher is distant and cold. We can access our Child Ego State too and have some spontaneous fun. However, we need to ensure that we are always laughing with and not at pupils. Choose Ego States thoughtfully. Some pupils will need more 'Nurturing Parent' (see Chapter 9). For example, you might notice that someone is looking ill or tired. You might look around the room and comment on the fact that the class looks a bit tired.

Show pupils that you as a teacher are human. Teachers make mistakes and when we make mistakes we can emphasise to pupils that the teacher is not perfect and is fallible like everyone else, but that we are still OK. Teachers do, however, need to be competent and in charge. Constant apologies will undermine their authority.

By using Ego States and apologising when we are wrong, we are modelling for pupils that teachers can change their behaviour and consequently they too can change their behaviour. We can show them that our classroom is a safe place where people are still OK even when they make mistakes and get things wrong. Be prepared as a teacher both to say sorry and to forgive. Change is difficult and if some pupils come from abusive backgrounds, they will be scared to admit that they are wrong.

Teachers can use praise and rewards throughout the lesson to show that they value both individuals and the whole class. Praise rather than punishment will motivate pupils to modify and change their behaviour.

Another way of developing relationships with pupils is to show an interest in the kinds of things which they might be interested in. As fans of football and pop music, we have both found these topics useful in forming and maintaining relationships. This does not mean that you suddenly have to go out and buy all the latest CDs or go and watch your local football team! It just means taking note of what is happening in the news so that you come across as approachable and not 'old-fashioned'.

It is amazing to see how much more motivated pupils can be if you find a topic which interests them and incorporate it in a creative way into your lesson. One of Sandra's PGCE students (Daniela Maurri) noticed how a boy who could not remember his French vocabulary had written out from memory, all of the lyrics to a complicated song by Nirvana. His memory was OK, so long as he was motivated to remember!

Finally, in all your relationships with pupils think about the way you would like to be treated. Show the pupils that you are flexible in both your thinking and behaviour but you are not weak. Do not allow pupils to deny your rights as a teacher. Yet, at the same time, think about the behaviour we have discussed in this chapter. You are the adult in the class and it is your job to set the standard of behaviour and work you want from the pupils. Relationships will help you to teach better and the class to learn more easily. This does not mean that you have to please all the pupils all of the time! Sometimes you have to accept that they will feel angry with you and this may be necessary for change.

It is worth remembering that relationships can only be built up over a period of time. This is why it is often difficult to manage behaviour in the early stages of a teacher's career or when taking over new groups. No relationships have been formed yet. Teachers who have been at a school for a number of years often come with a 'reputation'. In other words, pupils from previous years pass on the message about what that teacher is like. This can work to the teacher's advantage, but in the pupils' eyes, respect still has to be earned. It can also work to a teacher's detriment if former pupils are scathing about the teacher.

To summarise this section on relationships, both pupils and teachers often say that what they want in the classroom is mutual respect. 'Respect... is [another] Adult–Adult relation ... based upon straight talk and the fulfilment of social contracts ... Reliability and commitment together add up to trustworthiness and trust is what gives rise to respect' (Berne, 1973).

Part 3

Structuring the Lesson

Chapter 12
Time Structuring

...most people become very uneasy when they are faced with a period of unstructured time.

(Berne, 1991)

Berne said that whenever people get together, there are different ways in which they use or structure their time. Indeed, he believed that human beings have a 'hunger' for structuring their time. The main reasons that pupils misbehave in a classroom are not being able to do the work, fear of failure, boredom, lack of clarity about what to do, too long spent on an activity without a break, lack of self-esteem and poor relationships.

It follows, then, that if the teacher does not clearly structure the time in the lesson, then some pupils will use the time to be disruptive. Unstructured time gives out the message that nothing serious or important is going on. Pupils may then decide to structure time in their own way. Indeed, it is vital that teachers start and end their lessons on time, reinforcing the importance of time and role modelling how to do it.

Activity

Brainstorm your own ideas about time. What are the positive messages you want pupils to develop about using time in your classroom? Why is time important in your classroom? Make a list of how you allocate time in one of your lessons.

WHAT DO WE NEED TO TEACH PUPILS ABOUT TIME?

- Time is a precious and finite commodity.
- Time must not be wasted.
- Time is needed to learn new content and skills.
- Time is needed by everyone in order to be clever.
- Pupils need time to understand ideas and time to explain ideas.
- Time is needed for self-reflection and self assessment.
- Time is needed to set targets and celebrate successes in the classroom.
- There is no time in the lesson to make fun of or ridicule people.

- Finally there is enough time for everyone in the classroom to be heard and to succeed.

How did Berne suggest that we structure time to meet our 'hunger'? Berne suggested six ways in which people structure their time. These are:

- Withdrawal – the person is physically present, but does not interact with others
- Rituals – familiar social interactions which follow a set pattern
- Pastimes – talking about everyday events, chatting
- Activities – people direct their energy into achieving some goal or outcome
- Games – they get involved in a sequence of transactions which end up with them feeling bad
- Intimacy – they express their authentic feelings and personal needs to each other without censoring anything.

Let us look at some of these in the context of the classroom. In most cases, they can be used both positively and negatively

Withdrawal: Negative

When they have unstructured time, some pupils withdraw. In other words, they become silent. They avoid the risk of rejection by not engaging with others. These pupils find it difficult to bond with the other pupils or the teacher. They are often the quiet and sometimes invisible pupils. They do what they are told and do not misbehave; however, they never seem as if they are part of the lesson or the group. There can be a number of reasons for this. They may be very shy and lacking in confidence. They might possibly be victims of bullying.

It is good, therefore, to encourage pupils to talk in a safe environment. First of all, it is important that you and the pupils know exactly what the value of talking about ideas is. Explain to pupils that talking about ideas to someone else allows us to check our understanding of ideas. The actual process of talking helps us to realise that we are stuck or unclear about certain ideas.

One way of involving quiet pupils is to get them to share their ideas with their partner, so they might feel more willing to join in class discussions. It is worth realising that, for such a pupil, talking in front of the rest of the class can be very embarrassing. You might want to tell pupils that you would like everyone to join in discussion work, but as long as people are behaving and working hard you will not force anyone to talk in front of the class who does not want to do so.

Giving pupils the opportunity to start a problem page on which they can write down what they do not understand or things they want you to go over again is a way of opening a dialogue with withdrawn pupils. This can be a way of pupils making you aware that they do not understand as much as you thought or that your teaching style is not working.

Withdrawal: Positive

Teaching pupils the importance of withdrawing from the lesson for positive reasons is also important. Sometimes we want pupils to read in silence or to sit quietly and reflect on their feeling or thoughts.

Rituals: Negative

When we greet people, we are getting involved in ritual behaviour. We might enquire how they are, but really we do not want a list of all their ailments or problems. We are expecting a stereotypical answer such as 'I'm fine and how are you?'

Rituals: Positive

Rituals are the way in which the teacher introduces the class to how they want to structure time. Through Contracts, behaviour posters and modelling, the teacher makes it clear how time will be used.

Rituals in a classroom give pupils a predictable pattern; they allow them to feel safe because they know what to do. They do not have to guess what they have to do when they come into the room because there is a predictable pattern of behaviour that makes them feel more secure. They may get into the habit of entering the room, getting their books out ready for the lesson, greeting the teacher and answering the register. There may be regular 'slots' in the lesson which pupils get used to and even ask for if the teacher happens to forget.

Pastimes: Negative

When given an opportunity, pupils will end up talking about what happened last night or at the weekend, their favourite song, etc. They enjoy doing this, but it can be very disruptive.

Pastimes: Positive

Sometimes, talking about events can be integrated into the context of the lesson and linked to what the pupils are doing. In Modern Languages, for example, this is a great way to revise the past tense. You may be able to think of other ways appropriate to your subject that this could be used. Pastiming can also be a way of forming relationships or attaching to pupils. You may, for example, ask them about a school trip they have been on, or how their form did on Sports' Day.

Games: Negative

Pupils may get into Games with each other if their time is not carefully structured. This may take the form of name calling or stealing some else's equipment. They may even get into Games with the teacher and start an argument.

Intimacy: Positive

When pupils and teachers express their genuine feelings towards each other, they are being intimate. This may involve praising a pupil or the pupil telling the teacher that they enjoyed the lesson. This also happens when pupils disclose personal information in an appropriate way.

SHARING AND ORGANISING TIME

From our own experiences as teachers, we have come to realise that pupils do not like wasting time. Most pupils want to learn and they want to succeed. Therefore it is important to share the aims, or intended learning outcomes of the lesson with the pupils.

Imagine following someone with a map. You do not know where you are going and they refuse to share the map. You would feel angry and in the end you would go off on your own. You may have done this yourself as teachers on a course or a teacher may have done this to you.

We believe that pupils are more likely to work with the teacher and not waste time when they know what they are doing and why they are doing it. Writing the learning outcomes on the board and getting pupils to come out to the front and tick them off gives the pupils a feeling that they are sharing in a worthwhile, whole class experience. Giving the class a sheet with the content, key questions and skills they will cover over a half term allows them to see what they are learning. Another idea is to give examination groups a list of weeks and the work that needs covering in that time.

The teacher needs to tell pupils what the payoff and the rewards are of using their time properly. By sharing the outcomes, we are informing pupils where and how they will get their praise (Strokes). Pupils then do not have to go in search of attention, they know they will get it from the teacher.

By sharing the big picture of what the lesson is about, we are sending out messages to the class:

- What we are doing is important.
- We are being respectful.
- We are saying that this will only be successful if we work in partnership on this work.
- This is how you succeed.

Less able students often find it difficult to concentrate and focus their attention for any length of time. Therefore they need someone to organise time for them. If a pupil cannot access an activity, they will get involved in Games with other pupils or the teacher. Often this is a way to camouflage the fact they are having difficulty with the work. They need short and sharp instructions and activities broken down into clear manageable chunks that have an immediate outcome.

Organising work in terms of three levels can help: Level one – all pupils must complete this activity; level two – some pupils should manage to do this activity; level three – a few pupils could get this far. This does not mean we have to teach them inferior and second-rate work. Less able students may find it difficult writing their ideas down but they are capable of understanding quite complex ideas and developing sophisticated oral explanations. Sharing with a class your expectations of them at the start of a lesson can help the class to develop more self-esteem and consequently the whole class becomes more focused on the work. For example:

> This work is difficult but I know that when you work hard and concentrate you can produce clever work.

> With some groups I would not try such difficult work, however, I know you can do this work if you concentrate and do your best.

> I'm going to teach you the posh word for this idea. Why not impress another teacher by telling them that you know what … means?

We can make pupils aware of how much time they have to complete an activity. We can make them aware of how much time they have used up. It is important to give them time limits for an activity as this avoids them going 'off task'. It is also useful to count down the minutes to the end of an activity in order to bring them back to what they are doing. 'You have ten minutes left … five minutes … you are now in your last two minutes … only thirty seconds to go, 10, 9, … stop.'

You can also split the task up. You might say that they have two minutes to do one part of the activity and three minutes for the other part, then after two minutes, remind them 'You should now be getting on to the second part of the activity.' This is a useful technique for helping them to structure time in exams.

Also, you can write up an activity on the board and negotiate with pupils how much time they think each section of the work will take to complete.

Another way of structuring the time is to get pupils to share their work with other pupils. This way they have to complete their work for an audience other than the teacher.

Teachers need to teach pupils that time in their lessons is a valuable commodity. As teachers we need to be clear about how we use time and what messages we want pupils to know about how time is used in our classrooms.

Chapter 13
The Start of the Lesson

During the course of this book, we will be looking at a number of theories from Transactional Analysis psychotherapy that will be useful, as a means of both understanding as well as managing behaviour. However, we are aware that teachers are busy people and often want something practical that they can use straightaway in their classroom. Therefore we have divided the next part up into three sections, representing the three main parts of the lesson:

- the start of the lesson
- activities and ideas to use during the course of the lesson
- the end of the lesson.

Let us look, first of all, at how teachers can start a lesson. Below are a number of practical ideas that you can use and next to them are the relevant TA theories covered elsewhere in the book. There is no one set way of starting a lesson so you might use some ideas, and modify and reject others.

- *Arrive early*
  It is best to be in the room before the pupils arrive. Sometimes this is just not possible, due to room changes, covering colleagues in other areas of the school, being on duty, coming back from assembly, etc. However, this can set the tone for the rest of the lesson (see Chapter 8, Role Modelling.)
- *Arrange the seating*
  Arrange the seating in the room as you want it and in a way that minimises disruption. Experiment if you find that a particular seating arrangement is not working. You may also decide to impose a seating plan where certain pupils do not sit together, ensuring that you explain the reasons for this beforehand. You can also explain how they should behave in order to be allowed to revert to their old seating arrangements and sit next to their friends. (See Chapter 7, Contracts.)
- *Be organised*
  Make sure you have all the materials and resources you need before the lesson begins. Have work ready on the board or use an Overhead Projector to show pupils what they need to do. With difficult classes, do not turn your back on

them. Ensure all your materials are at hand and that you have enough of them. While you are looking for something, the class may well go off task and become difficult.

- *Get the pupils into the room as soon as possible*
  Leaving pupils waiting can lead to disruption in the corridors or outside.

- *Demonstrate your serious intentions to get the lesson started promptly*
  Get pupils doing something when they come in (see Chapter 12, Time Structuring). This should be something which they can do without help if possible. This leaves you free to monitor the entrance of the other pupils. You may, for example, have something ready on the board or a sheet on their desk, such as a word search. The register can then be taken in silence and books can be given out calmly. Pupils will be on task straight away.

- *Greet the pupils as they arrive*
  Use their names (see Chapter 6, Strokes). Ask pupils whether they have enjoyed the day or done something nice over the weekend. It is more difficult for most pupils to be badly behaved when someone has been nice and polite to them and has related to them as an individual. They will also be making an attachment to you (see Chapter 11, Relationships). In addition, pupils will be more likely to be positive towards you if you look enthusiastic or pleased to see them. Be positive about your subject and what you are teaching.

- *Insist on certain standards of behaviour as pupils enter the classroom*
  Praise those pupils who have their equipment out and are getting on with work straight away. Praise works better than punishment (see Chapter 6, Strokes).

- *Make them aware of your expectations*
  Make explicit what kind of behaviour you expect. Develop shared rules which are displayed in the room. Never speak to the class while they are talking, insist on silence when you talk. Wait if necessary, but make it clear what you are waiting for! Your body language should be congruent, reflecting the fact that you expect to get silence (see Chapter 7, Contracts). Insist that pupils put their hand up to ask or answer a question. Ask pupils to write down their behaviour target for the lesson. Tell them what rewards they can expect at the end of the lesson and tell them what you were pleased with last lesson.

- *Make students aware of the rewards and the punishments available*
  Make it clear that you are interested in teaching and you prefer to praise and reward students. If they misbehave, then they are *choosing* to be punished (see Chapter 19, Winners and Losers).

- *Know their names*
  It is vital to learn pupils' names as quickly as possible, These can be used both to show that you care about them as an individual and as a technique for managing behaviour. We pointed out how important it is for pupils to get attention (see Chapter 6, Strokes). Think about how you feel when someone forgets your name or gets it wrong.

- *Take the register*
  Most schools insist on teachers taking a register every lesson. This is to check on truancy, as a reference for parents' evening so you know what work a pupil may have missed and as a way of monitoring missing homework. Use the register as a way of greeting each pupil individually, rather than a mundane list read out in a monotone voice (Hunger Recognition). Using the numbers on the register and asking pupils to call out their number to indicate their presence is dehumanising.

- *Share your intended learning outcomes*
  Share the learning outcomes with the pupils to give a sense of shared ownership. One of Sandra's PGCE students (Liz Stringer) always used the phrase 'Was lernen wir heute mit Frau Stringer?' (What are we going to learn today with Mrs Stringer?) The emphasis on the word 'with' helps pupils to develop a sense of shared ownership. Sharing the intended learning outcomes is best done both verbally and in written form so that pupils have a visual way of monitoring where they are up to in the lesson and checking off what has been done. Aim to make pupils aware of what they need to do as quickly as possible. Less able pupils will find it difficult to listen for a long period of time.

  Put the lesson into context by relating the work to what has been covered previously and what will follow in future lessons. Remember to give clear instructions. Get pupils in pairs to check that they know what to do and then ask one of them to explain what the class needs to do or offer reward (House point/card, etc.) for anyone who can tell the class (see Chapter 6, Strokes).

- *Read the Individual Education Plans (IEPs) and notes about pupils with Special Educational Needs (SEN)*
  These may have implications for pupils' behaviour or potential difficulties in the lesson. Do not prejudge pupils based on what you have read about them, but at the same time be pre-warned of their learning difficulties, ability to grasp certain ideas, challenging behaviour or triggers to such behaviour. Some pupils, for example, do not like being asked questions directly or are worried about reading out aloud in front of the rest of the class.

  Start off each lesson with the idea that the individual is OK, can think and can change (see Chapter 2, Philosophical Assumptions in TA).

- *Use differentiation in your lesson*
  Think about how you are going to have to break down the work, structure it and support the less able students in the class. You may want to think about differentiation of activities and materials in terms of:
  - must (all pupils must complete this work)
  - should (most pupils should complete this part)
  - could (some pupils could finish this part).

Another way of doing this is to use the model of:
- core (everyone does this)
- extension (more able pupils will do this)
- support (less able pupils will need this to help them).

Have work sheets that are differentiated. There will be some pupils who might take five minutes over an activity whilst another pupil might take 15 minutes. Have reference or support materials available for pupils who have difficulties with reading and writing.

Always have extension activities prepared for the more able pupils as they too can misbehave given unstructured time. Do not wait for these pupils to say 'I've finished that, what should I do now?' Make sure they know in advance.

- *Be polite and model good behaviour and ways of treating people right from the start.*

Finally, if necessary, have an arrangement, set up in advance with another teacher (usually in the same department) to send a troublesome pupil to. It is more effective if they go to a group where the pupils are either much younger (peer groups often provide an audience) or are well behaved (so they can role model good behaviour).

One year 9 boy who was sent to Sandra as Head of Department nearly every lesson due to disruptive behaviour in French, eventually joined a very able group full-time and started to join in the lesson sensibly. He had had good behaviour modelled for him by the other pupils and then started to get his attention and Strokes for good behaviour and effort, rather than misbehaviour.

The start of the lesson is important as it sets the tone for what follows. Using these ideas will help you to manage it more effectively, while at the same time keeping pupils on task.

Chapter 14
The Middle of the Lesson

A desperate teacher asks 'What can I do with this lot for the next 20 minutes?' Ideally, a teacher will always plan activities bearing in mind shifts of energy, but at times even this is not enough. It could be connected with the time of day (is it before lunch?), the previous lesson (did they have PE?) or the interest in the topic for that lesson.

Some of the problems and opportunities for this middle part of the lesson are:

- noticing the way a class feels
- bringing the class together to refocus them
- injecting pace and urgency
- checking that all pupils have understood the key ideas and skills of the lesson.

NOTICING THE WAY A CLASS FEELS

If you notice that pupils appear to be 'off task' or lacking in energy and purpose, you might ask them to put their pens down and then comment on the lack of urgency, effort or work from the class. Depending on your relationship with the group, you may ask them if there is a problem. It might be that the room is too hot or too cold (physical comfort is important) or the work is too difficult or too easy.

BRINGING THE CLASS TOGETHER TO REFOCUS THEM

Again, get the pupils to stop what they are doing, ask them if they are having difficulties, explain the task again and remind them of the purpose of the work. You might then set the pupils a target or challenge for the next ten minutes: 'In ten minutes I expect these things to be done. I will give rewards to anyone who can finish the work.' Within that ten minutes you can make them aware of the time they have left by counting down (see Chapter 12, Time Structuring)

You have just had two minutes.
Five minutes left.
Down to the last two minutes.

INJECTING PACE AND URGENCY

Sometimes during the middle of the lesson there can be a loss of pace. This is an opportunity to inject some pace. Use the idea of 'settle and stir'. If they have just had a task which settles them, such as writing, then set them a 'stirring task' such as a game, brainstorming, pairwork, groupwork or a survey. Preferably something which gets them moving around the classroom to disperse the energy in the room. Boys in particular like activities which involve movement. This also ensures that different learning styles are catered for.

You could also get pupils to mark each other's work so far. This means that there is pressure on the pupils rather than the teacher. It gives pupils a chance to get attention and Strokes. Write a mark scheme on the board or develop one at the start of the lesson. Pupils can swap books and then they can write one thing they liked about the work and one about how to improve. Emphasise that they must be positive and discuss the types of comments that are and are not acceptable. Pupils can then nominate another pupil's work for a card and praise. The 'how to improve' comments can be written up on the board and these can be ideas that pupils who have finished can use to improve or redraft their own work (see Chapter 8, Role Modelling).

Choose pupils who have completed work and get them to walk around and nominate other pupils for praise or cards. Get them to note things they like about the class's work and then they can report back to the class. Give them ground rules, they are not to comment on anything negative or touch anyone's equipment or work.

CHECKING WHETHER ALL PUPILS HAVE GRASPED KEY IDEAS AND SKILLS

At this point of the lesson you can make pupils aware of how much time they have left and where they should be in terms of the work. You can tick off objectives on the board and give individuals or the whole class praise for the work they have done so far.

You can ask pupils to write down three things that they think everyone should have learnt so far. You can make it into a game by giving points to ideas that are offered. This appeals to the competitive nature of some pupils.

You can remind them what they need to achieve in the second half of the lesson.

You can inject some humour by giving a half-time report football style about the class's performance.

Teachers usually manage the start and end of the lesson efficiently, but sometimes there is a need to think about how to maintain the momentum in the middle of the lesson.

Chapter 15

The End of the Lesson

It is important that lessons end on time with pupils packed up and ready to go (see Chapters 8 and 12, Role Modelling and Time Structuring). Pupils get angry if they are late leaving the room. This may be because it is break time and they want to meet their friends, or because it is lunch-time and they are hungry. Their leisure time is important, as they do need time to recharge their batteries and 'let off steam'. They may also be keen to get to their next lesson (which could be on the other side of the school) on time.

If it is necessary to keep pupils behind for any reason, remember the 'thirty second rule'. This states that if a pupil is being told off, they will stop listening after 30 seconds, so a five-minute tirade about how bad their behaviour has been will have little or no effect.

Nor is it a good idea to give out rewards after the end of the lesson. First, it is as if they are being punished for doing something well and, second, they should receive their praise and rewards in front of the rest of the class in order to highlight the importance of good work and behaviour. It is best to use private reprimand and public praise.

It is always a good idea to ensure that everyone leaves the lesson with the opportunity to feel OK. You cannot make somebody feel OK, but you can create a situation in which they can move to an OK position. This might mean, for example, saying that you are not pleased with the way they have behaved in that lesson, suggest ways in which they can improve and then say how you look forward to seeing the changes in them. Again, this should be done concisely in 30 seconds.

> I am not happy with the fact that you have been disrupting Peter today. Next lesson you will sit away from him and show me that you can behave. Do you understand why? I know that you are a sensible pupil who can do well in this subject and will make the necessary changes. I look forward to seeing you show me what you can do. Have a good weekend. Good bye.

In the last part of the lesson, the teacher should do the following things:

- *Return to the intended learning outcomes and check what pupils have learnt*
  A plenary session is important. This can be done in lots of different ways. The teacher can ask the whole class to say three things they have learnt in the lesson.

The teacher can ask the individual pupils to write down in their books three things they have learnt, then share them with a partner and then feedback to the whole group. The teacher can use a game or an activity to check what they have learnt.

- *Set the homework*
  If the pupils are due to be given homework, it should be given to them well before the end of the lesson. They should be told what it is verbally and it should also be written on the board. It should be clear what is expected of them, how to get help or support (reference materials, notes or dictionaries), when the deadline is and how much you expect them to do. It should also be differentiated.

- *Collect in all materials such as text books, worksheets, glue, felt tips, rulers, etc.*
  Make sure that this is well organised. Perhaps choose sensible pupils to collect them in. Ensure you know how many there are so that nothing goes missing.

- *Leave the room tidy*
  You may be teaching in your own room or you may not. Whichever the case, ensure that the room is tidy before the next group comes in, otherwise this will set the tone for the next group. You need to clean the board, put away all materials, check the floor for litter (check each row of chairs and ask each person to pick up anything which is under their desk) and ask pupils to put their chairs under the desks neatly. This is also important for Health and Safety. (Pupils coming in may trip over chairs which are sticking out.)

- *Dismiss the pupils in an orderly fashion*
  Do not just say 'OK, off you go', there could be pandemonium! The best way to dismiss a group is to let a different row go first each time and dismiss them row by row. You should never dismiss them according to 'girls first' as this is poor role modelling and stereotyping. It is also unfair.

  A concluding remark with a positive message is also a good idea. 'You have worked well today, well done!' Or, 'I was disappointed with the way you came into the room, but since then you have produced some good work.' Ending the lesson on a positive note sends pupils away feeling good about themselves, in a positive frame of mind for the following lesson and looking forward(!) to their next lesson with you.

Part 4

Maintaining Relationships in the Classroom

Chapter 16

Life Scripts

*...a personal life plan which an individual decides upon at an early age
in reaction to her interpretation of both external and internal events.*
(Woollams and Brown, 1978)

Berne put forward the theory that at an early age (usually about two or three),
children make decisions about themselves and the world they live in, based on
messages they receive from their parents or primary caretakers. It is almost as if the
child has written its own script for life, like a play to be acted out throughout their
life.

These messages from parents may be verbal or non-verbal, direct or indirect. They
may be given through role modelling (the child copies the parent's behaviour),
labelling (the parent tells the child that they are naughty, clever, irritating, etc.) or
through suggestion (the parents indirectly indicate what they want them to do).

At the time when the children made these decisions, it was the only way they had
of getting their needs met and getting Strokes, so they adapted their behaviour in
order to survive in the family. The child's script will dictate the way they see
themselves (their Life Position), other people and the world. It will affect the role or
roles they are willing to play in life and their patterns of behaviour.

An important thing to remember is that the way the child receives these messages
may vary. This is why siblings do not necessarily have the same Life Script. They may
choose to interpret the message in a particular way and behave accordingly.

The advantage of a script is that it makes life predictable. The person always
knows what they should say or how they ought to behave. The downside of living a
script is that an individual's behaviour lacks spontaneity and they are not
autonomous. It is as if a person has been programmed like a robot to behave in a
predictable way. The script can therefore be limiting.

As a person grows up they have the potential to move out of script: to exist in the
here and now and use the resources they now have as an adult to solve problems
and get their needs met.

One way of finding out what a person's script may be is to ask them to complete
these sentences:

I am the sort of person who ....

Life is ……………………….......

Other people are ………………..

The script decision can be written in this way:

I am ………..., other people are ………..., the world is ………..., and so I will …………….

In this chapter we aim to give an overview of the theory of Life Scripts. We would therefore recommend that if you want a more detailed discussion on this subject you refer to the bibliography.

WHY DO TEACHERS NEED TO KNOW ABOUT LIFE SCRIPTS?

In a busy classroom, teachers do not have the time or the expertise to identify different script issues and help each individual to understand and move out of their script. However, some knowledge of how children produce their Life Scripts and how teachers can affect a Life Script can be very useful in a classroom.

This can help the teacher to understand why a pupil has adopted a negative Life Position and it can also help them to use strategies that will enable the pupils to update their view of themselves. Teachers can help pupils to learn more positive ways of relating both to themselves and to other people. Pupils can be invited to move towards OKness (Woollams and Brown, 1978). This will encourage some pupils to develop a sense of their own OKness and begin to move out of their particular negative script.

ACTIVITY

Let us look at two examples of pupils' Life Scripts. As you read the two examples below decide what the scripts of the girls are. Think about how these scripts are limiting both individuals. Try to think of any strategies you could use to move these girls into an OK position.

Jane feels she has to please people in order to be OK. She always does what her teachers ask. Jane likes to get things right and so she spends far too much time on her homework. Consequently she is often tired because she spends so much of her time pleasing other people or worrying about what other girls might think of her. Jane never gets angry, but she does feel depressed.

Sally sees herself as bad. Her life position is 'I'm not OK, you're not OK'. As a child, her father told her that she was bad and she is made the scapegoat for many of her family's problems. Sally is always in trouble at school. She has been involved in incidents of bullying and she often gets involved in fights. Recently Sally told the Headteacher that she didn't care what he thought of her.

What conclusions can we come to about the girls' Life Scripts? Jane believes that she can only be OK if she pleases other people. Her Life Position is 'I'm not OK, you're OK'. She feels that she can only be OK with other people if she pleases them by being perfect. Sally defends against not feeling OK by being strong and persecuting other people. Her Life Position is 'I'm not OK, you're not OK'.

Neither of these girls is developing their true potential. Their behaviour is repetitive and not flexible. The girls do not seem to be able to adapt or change their behaviour. Their scripts do not solve problems; in fact, their scripts create problems. Both girls are trapped in the past. Old messages about how they should behave continually play in their heads. Each girl is prompted and motivated by her own script. However, much of their script is outside of their awareness. Their scripts have created a world of fear and lack of communication. These girls are not even communicating with themselves. There is a lack of choice in their behaviour. It is compulsive. The girls need to update their scripts by challenging their beliefs and using the Adult resources they now have at their disposal to solve their problems.

HOW DID THESE GIRLS DEVELOP THEIR SCRIPTS?

The girls, as we pointed out earlier, would have made decisions at an early age about what their script should be. Parents would have given these girls script messages. In the case of Sally we can see that she was told at an early age that she was bad.

Parents can give messages to children at an early age about how they should see themselves and how they should behave. These messages can be given in a number of ways:

- modelling
- commands
- attributions
- injunctions
- drivers
- permissions.

Modelling

The Parent may not say anything directly to the child about physical contact but a child can sense from lack of physical contact that getting close to other people is not

OK. In another family a parent may get their own way by sulking and a child makes the decision that sulking is the best way of getting what you want in life.

Commands

Parents can give children commands that tell them exactly how they should behave. Whether a child decides to incorporate the command into their script depends on how often the command is given and the way that it is given.

- Boys don't cry.
- Don't give up.
- Do what I say.
- Hurry up.

Attributions

Parents tell children what they should be like. They attribute them with certain characteristics.

- You always get things wrong. You are useless.
- You are good at adding up. You are clever.
- You are just like your Auntie (good/bad).

Injunctions

Bob and Mary Goulding (1979) identified twelve injunctions. An Injunction is a negative script message that is stored in the Child Ego State. It usually starts with the expression 'Don't'. Remember that this was probably not said directly to the child, but suggested. For example: on numerous occasions during her early childhood, Sally's father told her that she was bad. Jane was constantly told that being angry was wrong. She should be a good girl and do what her parents told her to do.

- *Don't exist*
  This may fit the child who is invisible in a class.
- *Don't be you*
  Jane is an example of a girl who is affected by this injunction.
- *Don't be a child*
  In some families the child ends up mothering or fathering the parent. You also notice some children with older parents are little adults rather than children.
- *Don't grow up*
  You get parents still wanting to make decisions for their 22-year-old son or daughter.

- *Don't make it*
  Some parents do not want their children to do better than them. Sometimes you see working-class parents worried that their clever child will outgrow them and leave them behind if they go to university. The parent outside of their consciousness does all they can do to stop their child from succeeding.
- *Don't (don't do anything)*
  This is an injunction given by a parent who does too much for their child. This child grows up into a man or woman who can do nothing for themselves.
- *Don't be important*
  You notice some teachers who do brilliant work but never tell anyone else in the school about it.
- *Don't belong*
  Pupils who find it difficult to mix and do not have any friends. Sally in our example finds it difficult to be part of school life.

Other injunctions include

- Don't be close.
- Don't be well.
- Don't think.
- Don't feel. Sally is being strong so she does not have to feel her sadness.

Drivers

When we are in stressful situations we will revert to what in TA is called 'Driver Behaviour'. Driver behaviour dictates how we will behave. It is the behaviour that we exhibit just before we go into our own particular script. There are five drivers:

- Be perfect.
- Please other people.
- Try hard.
- Be strong.
- Hurry up.

Drivers are another set of messages which people gave us in the past about the way we should behave. On a surface level they may seem acceptable ways of teaching someone how to behave. For example, a parent may tell their child to do something again because it is not right. If this message is consistently given to the child again and again, then they may come to the conclusion that they are only OK if they get things perfectly right. In Jane's case, she is driven by 'Please other people'. She feels that she has to get things right in order to please other people.

Drivers control a person's behaviour and they result in restrictive ways of behaving. The person who wants to do a perfect job will do excellent work but they may take too long or they may drive themselves so hard that they become ill. The person is a prisoner to their Driver. When under pressure the only way for this person to be OK is to maintain their Driver behaviour. The problem is that no one can maintain their Driver behaviour for 24 hours a day (Jane cannot please everyone she comes across during a day). When an individual fails to maintain their Driver behaviour they collect their script 'pay-off'. In Jane's case she feels that when she upsets other people she is not OK.

We can see the Driver messages in the two girls' behaviour. Sally's Driver behaviour is 'Be strong', while Jane's Driver behaviour is 'Please other people'. Driver behaviour is an attempt to get attention and recognition from other people. Jane and Sally both use their Driver behaviour just before they go into script.

Permissions

These are positive messages received from the parents. They include permission to:

- exist
- have basic needs
- feel emotions
- think
- be close
- be their own age
- succeed.

You can see that these permissions are the opposite of the negative messages known as injunctions. Again, you need to remember that these messages may not be given verbally or even directly.

WHAT CAN WE, AS TEACHERS, REALISTICALLY DO ABOUT SCRIPTS IN THE CLASSROOM?

We cannot give counselling or psychotherapy to our pupils. What we can do is provide an environment in which we teach pupils how to access their Adult resources in order to solve problems. Below are examples of how teachers can help some pupils to move out of their scripts:

- They can encourage them to become aware of their strengths.
- They can use Strokes to help them develop their confidence and self-esteem.
- They can give pupils permission to try new ways of behaving and relating to themselves and other people.
- They can create an atmosphere of trust, care and safety in which each pupil feels accepted as an individual person.

By doing these things, the teacher is creating an environment in which pupils are given the opportunity to begin to break free of negative scripting.

We can help pupils to avoid their own Driver behaviour by focusing on the good things they are doing and inviting them to operate from an I'm OK, you're OK Life Position.

With pupils who are clearly driven by 'Be perfect', teachers can give them permission to make mistakes. We can, as teachers, model for them how mistakes are sometimes an opportunity to learn something new. Pupils can have a page in their books where they can write down things they do not understand or questions they want answered. Around our classroom we can have names of people who did things wrong yet were later hailed as geniuses. We can teach pupils not to be judgmental towards themselves or other people.

Those pupils who have 'Don't exist' or 'Don't be important' injunctions can be taught through Contracts that everyone has rights and everyone has the right to be treated respectfully by other people. By seeing their teacher using Strokes and learning self-stroking, they can begin to see that success is something that they can achieve.

With pupils who have 'Don't be close' injunctions they can learn through group work or drama that they can work with other pupils and share feelings and be safe.

It is worth noting that for some pupils messages they were given about how they should behave were used as a defence against a more threatening outcome. For example, 'If I don't exist in this family no one can abuse me.' If we encourage them to give up the protection they feel they need from not existing, we may leave them open to much more frightening feelings.

In a classroom we are not giving pupils therapy; what we are attempting to do is give them opportunities to relate to themselves and other people more positively. Some pupils may be ready to take these opportunities to grow, while other pupils may feel too stuck or scared to accept them. Therefore, we must remember as teachers to be sensitive to the needs of pupils as individuals.

In their book *Born to Win* (1996) Muriel James and Dorothy Jongeward write about Cultural Scripts. We see the world through the eyes of a particular group of people or nation. Some pupils will come from a particular ethnic group and it will be important for them to maintain their cultural and religious beliefs. Their cultural scripting may involve us as teachers needing to understand their culture/religion, so they feel that it is being respected and consequently they can feel OK in our classrooms.

If we study pupils in a school, pupils will have Peer Group Scripts. Boys may see getting on and doing well as not 'cool'. Some boys may come from home backgrounds where women are treated in an inferior, disrespectful and sexist manner; teaching these types of boys is going to be more difficult for women. Seeing behaviour as programmed behaviour rather than behaviour of choice does help the teacher to realise that it is not a personal attack. It also helps us to empathise with difficult pupils because we can begin to realise how the pupil is a product of their script. Such pupils are victims of their script; they are unable to make choices because they do not have any awareness and are controlled by their script.

Teachers can become aware of their own script too. If you have a feeling of 'this always happens to me' or 'I never get what I want', then you may need to look at your own script. You might notice how you create stress for yourself by wanting to be perfect or you might notice how you miss out on promotion because you feel you are not important. If you are driven by the 'Hurry up' Driver, you may feel as if you have to cram lots of information into one lesson and have to teach everything very fast if you are to fit in all the work you want to cover. Pupils may find it hard to understand ideas because you rush through topics too fast.

Other ways of recognising script behaviour is through the following:

- Breathing (the person may sigh).
- Body language (this may suddenly become guarded or the person may use certain gestures).
- Accent (the person may even adopt the accent of the person who originally gave them the message).
- Tone of voice (the voice may suddenly become very weak or very powerful).
- The words used (these may seem inappropriate or incongruous).
- The type of laughter (this may be 'gallows' laughter, i.e. inappropriate).

Everyone in the classroom, both pupils and teachers, can begin to change their script, once they are made aware of it.

It is difficult, in the midst of conflict, for a teacher to be compassionate towards the pupil who is annoying them but it is important to realise that pupils are products of their particular script in the same way we all are. Their script may be more harmful and difficult to live out than our own scripts. They may have uncaring parents or abusive parents. Some pupils may have inadequate parents and they end up being the parent in the family. As teachers we are not always fully aware of the difficult home backgrounds of all our pupils. We cannot overestimate the effect which family upbringing may have had on pupils. As a result, the following things are starting to happen:

- Schools are introducing home–school agreements.
- Schools are making parents aware of the nature of their Personal and Social Development Courses and inviting them along to information evenings about the topics involved.
- The government is recommending parents of young offenders to attend parenting classes.

While most parents strive to do their best for their children and some intuitively 'do the right thing', parenting skills do not come naturally. Indeed, many parents copy what was role modelled for them by their own parents, which could include abuse and neglect. We understood this better when we attended courses on Adoption with Shropshire County Council and felt that all would-be parents would benefit from attending such courses. We transferred the skills we learnt to the classroom situation and found them extremely effective.

Chapter 17

Games

Games are sets of ulterior transactions, repetitive in nature, with a well defined psychological payoff.

(Berne, 1991)

Julie Hay (1993) suggests that Games are more accurately defined as 'psychological games' which are 'unconsciously programmed ways of behaving that result in repetitive interactions with others leading to negative pay-offs'.

ACTIVITY

Do you feel that there are some pupils with whom, however hard you try to get on with them, you always end up arguing? How do you feel? Do you feel angry, sad, confused, misunderstood? Do you feel like a Victim or a Persecutor?

With some pupils we allow ourselves to be sucked into repetitive ways of transacting with them. Before the lesson we might decide not to get angry, to stay calm and be in Adult. However, within minutes of being in the classroom we can find ourselves drawn into conflict with the pupils and we can feel confused about why this happened. There is a feeling of 'this is happening again'. We have been involved in a 'Game'.

The teacher sits at the desk with Beth marking her work. This is the second year Beth has been in this particular teacher's class.

Teacher: This is good but you tend to rush through some of the work.

Beth: You never like my work.

Teacher: When did I say I didn't like your work?

Beth: You didn't like my work in Year 8. You never like my work.

Teacher: I don't know where this has come from.

We probably start the Game thinking that we will get positive Strokes, 'I'll make an effort to get on with Beth' but then there is a moment of confusion. The Game ends up causing us and the pupil bad feelings and resentment. In classrooms Games prevent people from operating from an 'I'm OK, you're OK' position. They stop open communication and make it difficult for the teacher to develop a relationship with the pupil.

There are three levels of Games. First degree Games are socially acceptable and mainly involve discomfort. These are the main types which take place in the classroom. Second degree Games may involve breaking the law, no permanent irreversible damage occurs, but they are not socially acceptable and are often secretive. Third degree Games involve self-harm, injury to others, imprisonment or even death. (They end up in the surgery, the courtroom or the morgue.)

GAMES PUPILS PLAY?

Pupils have favourite Games which help to reinforce their script beliefs about themselves and other people. Therefore it is important to identify them and work out strategies for dealing with them. In order not to get into a Game, we have first to spot the Game and then make sure we do not join in. As teachers, we need to be using our Adult Ego State in order to spot a game and then stay out of it. Below are examples of Games pupils play in the classroom.

- Kick me
- Make me work/behave
- No one tells me what to do
- Now I've got you, you son of a bitch
- I'm only trying to help you
- See how hard I've tried and I still fail
- Yes but
- I'll fail myself before you have a chance to fail me
- If it weren't for you
- No one likes our family
- You never told me
- Poor Me
- I'm useless

Some teachers will discount their own power to deal with these Games. Instead of using strategies to successfully deal with them, they will shout, feel sorry for themselves, worry and be fearful or put up with the situation.

Stephen Karpman (1968) devised the Drama Triangle as a way of analysing games. He identifies three roles people play in games: Victim, Rescuer and Persecutor. People tend to move between the three roles (see Figure 17.1). The Drama Triangle in Figure 17.1 shows how pupils and teachers might move between the Victim, Rescuer and Persecutor positions in the classroom.

Persecutor
This is the person who is sarcastic, puts people down, is critical, moaning, bossy and controlling.

Rescuer
This is the person who says, 'I'll help, let me do it (for you), don't worry', etc.

Victim
This is the person who whines, 'I can't, poor me, what can I do, it's all my fault', etc.
   Let us now look at a Game that some pupils use in a classroom.

I'm useless (Poor Me)

Brian: This is doing my head in. I will never understand this

           (Here Brian is in Victim position and he is discounting his ability to solve the problem. He wants someone to rescue him.)

Teacher: You don't seem to know how to do this, Brian. Last week you found it difficult. Let me do this one for you.

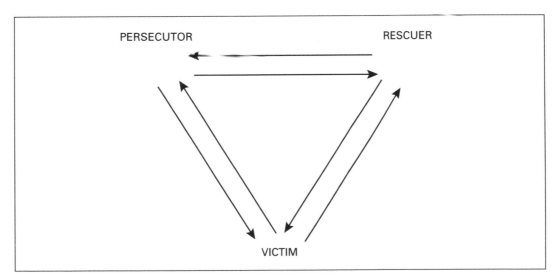

Figure 17.1   The Drama Triangle
Note: The drama triangle was developed by Dr. Stephen B. Karpman and first published in 'Fairy Tales and Script Drama Analysis,' *Transactional Analysis Bulletin* 7(26), pp. 39-43. It is reprinted here with the permission of Dr Karpman and the International Transactional Analysis Association.

(The teacher has become Rescuer. They are reinforcing Brian's helpless position of 'I'm not OK'.)

Brian: You go too fast and you don't explain things properly.

            (Brian has moved from Victim to Persecutor.)

Teacher: I was only trying to help.

            (The teacher has shifted positions from Rescuer to Victim.)

Brian moves from Victim to Persecutor.

Berne (1991) who originally suggested the idea of Games said that they go through a sequence of six stages. 'Whatever fits this formula is a game, whatever does not fit is not a game' (Berne, 1991). The formula of a game is:

Con + Gimmick = Response → Switch → Cross-up → Pay-off (Formula G)

The Con (ulterior invitation)
We might see Brian's Con in his body language. He may well have looked de-energised and been slouching in his chair. The teacher responds to Brian's outburst but does not see the ulterior message that lies behind what Brian says, 'You can try to help me but no one can. I am useless.' At this point the teacher needed to challenge this but the teacher was too concerned with rescuing Brian.

The Gimmick
(This is the weakness in the other person or the need to respond to the Con. The teacher buys into Brian's Con and reveals his Gimmick – his weak spot. 'I want to rescue my pupils' (Negative, Nurturing Parent Ego State).

The Response
Here the teacher responds to Brian's request for help (which we know is an attempt to reinforce his sense of failure).

The Switch
This is a shift. The teacher helps but Brian says he doesn't want the teacher's help. Brian has moved from Victim to Persecutor.

Cross-up
The teacher is confused, they thought they were helping, but Brian is angry. Things are not turning out the way they thought. The teacher now moves from Rescuer to Victim.

The Pay-off

(Both 'players' collect a bad pay-off.) Both Brian and the teacher get racket feelings (feelings that do not help to solve a problem). The teacher feels that they are a bad, failing teacher – their best is not good enough. Brian feels that he is useless and beyond any help a teacher could give.

KEY IDEAS ABOUT GAMES

- Games always end up with players experiencing feelings that will not help to solve the problem. In TA these are called racket feelings – inadequacy, sadness, fear, anger. Both Brian and his teacher ended up with racket feelings.
- Games involve an exchange of ulterior transactions between the players. Brian asking for help was actually asking the teacher to reinforce and underline his own feeling of inferiority and inadequacy. The teacher by helping Brian was emphasising that he rescued pupils.
- Games are always played without Adult awareness. The teacher was inviting Brian to make him aware of his own feelings of inadequacy as a teacher. Both Brian and the teacher used this Game to reinforce their own feelings of being misunderstood and undervalued.
- Games always include a moment of surprise or confusion. The teacher was hurt and upset. He thought he was helping Brian.

WHY DID BRIAN WANT TO PLAY A GAME?

There are several reasons for playing the Game.

- In Brian's case he used the Game to defend himself against feelings he did not want to feel, in this case, his own feelings of inadequacy. A pupil who storms out of the room in anger might be using it to defend against the fear of humiliation at being a poor reader.
- Brian's Game was a familiar way for him to behave. It always ends up in him and some of his teachers feeling bad but he knows what to do. There is a certainty about which role he and the teacher play and how they play it. The Game emphasises their Life Position – Brian was 'I'm not OK, you're not OK'.
- Pupils may not know another way of behaving or resolving conflict in a more productive way. When Brian is scared or unsure he only knows how to play Victim or Persecutor.
- To reinforce their script to support their frame of reference. In the case of Sally (see Life Scripts) she saw herself as a bad person. Therefore she got involved in Games to support her Life Position – 'I'm not OK, you're not OK'. The Game has reinforced her script. Brian has used the Game to support his Life Position.

- To satisfy fundamental needs (hungers). Pupils who do not get enough recognition will get involved in Games in order to get attention. The Game generates Strokes and negative Strokes are better than no Strokes.
- For stimulation. If the lesson is boring or not challenging a pupil, then they may get involved in a Game with the teacher as a means of creating excitement.
- If a teacher does not put enough pace into the lesson or leaves the pupils with lots of free time, they may use Games to structure this time.
- Games generate racket feelings. For example, a pupil who always gets argumentative and aggressive might be unconsciously doing this to hide their fear of looking stupid in front of the rest of the class.
- Games are an attempt to get our needs met. Pupils who sulk believe that they will get the teacher to give in and do what they want
- They give pupils an opportunity to collect Stamps (bad feelings) which can be cashed in later. The pupil who sulks in silence and feels that they are never listened to can wait for the day when the teacher is unfair and does not listen to them. They can then shout at that teacher and accuse them righteously of never listening to them.

HOW CAN TEACHERS DEAL WITH GAMES?

Catch the Game at the start

Teacher: Brian, you seem to have a problem. What do you want me to do to help you?

See how the teacher is not reinforcing Brian's Life Position. He is saying, 'You are OK in my eyes. I believe you have the intelligence to sort this problem. I will give you help but I will not rescue you.'

Teachers need to be aware of their own Gimmick, the weak spot that hooks them into a pupil's Game. If you are a Rescuer, you need to realise that rescuing other people does not work. Rescuing does not work because the person you are rescuing is put into a position of 'You are not OK, I am OK – that's why I had to rescue you'.

Don't accept discounting from students

Brian: This is doing my head in, I will never understand this.

Teacher: Brian, you do have the ability to solve this problem, however, you will have to think.

If you get sucked into a Game, you can refuse to take the bad feeling, the pay-off

Brian: You go too fast and you don't explain things properly.

Instead of feeling hurt, angry or sad, the teacher can think about what has happened. 'Well done, I've identified a Game. Now I'll know how to stop this next time.' The teacher does not wallow in bad feelings and self-pity, instead they give themselves a positive feeling for realising what Game they were playing. Now moving out of bad feeling, the teacher can move to intimacy with Brian. 'Brian, you seem to be angry with me'.

Give more Strokes

The teacher can give Brian more Strokes in the lesson so that he feels that he doesn't need to get into playing Games.

Access the Adult Ego State

Games are subjective and irrational. Both parties involved in the Game are not consciously aware of the rules. Therefore the teacher has to continually deal with the objective facts. The teacher needs to be able to access their Adult Ego State. Using Contracts, the teacher can be open with the pupil about the rules and behaviour expected in the classroom. This makes it harder for pupils to play Games such as, 'Make me work/behave', 'No one tells me what to do', 'You never told me' and 'Now I've got you, you son of a bitch' (commonly shortened to NIGYSOB).

Model good behaviour

By modelling good behaviour the teacher is only demanding from the pupil what they demand from themselves. This makes it more difficult for the pupil to play games such as 'You always pick on me'.

Do not get drawn into attacking the pupil

Deal with the behaviour or the Game and do not get drawn into attacking the pupil. This strategy will stop Games such as 'Nobody likes me'.

Jean: You don't like me, that is why you pick on me.

Teacher: I don't like you calling out in my lesson.

Jean: How do you know it was me?

Teacher: Jean, you were calling out. I am not wasting any more teaching time. If you think I am being unfair, see me at the end of the lesson. You were calling out. Stop it. Thank you.

Jean: I didn't shout out.

Teacher: You called out and I will see you at the end of lesson if you want to discuss it.

If the pupil continues, then the teacher will have to move her out of the lesson into a colleague's lesson. Here the teacher is using the 'broken record' technique. The teacher has the fact that Jean shouts out at the centre of the dispute and has not been drawn into Jean's Game by reminding her of the central issue, that of calling out. The teacher is also staying in Adult and reminding Jean of the objective fact that she shouted out. The teacher then gives Jean an option to speak to them at the end of lesson if she still feels she was unfairly treated. Jean's aim was to make the teacher not OK but the teacher stayed out of Jean's Game and did not persecute her.

If Jean had continued the argument and she had been moved to another lesson, she would have found it difficult to maintain her Game and would have gone into her racket feeling. When the teacher confronted Jean at the end of the lesson, they could have remained calm and dealt with the objective fact that they do not allow people to call out in their lesson. In this example, the teacher has not allowed Jean's behaviour to move them from 'I'm OK' to 'I'm not OK'. Jean can be reminded that she was given the option of discussing the matter calmly at the end of the lesson. Jean can then be asked or told what she can do to put this right next time and the consequences if it happens again.

ACTIVITY

Look at the example of a Game below. What seems to be Lee's Game? What mistakes does the teacher make in dealing with Lee? How would you deal with it?

Teacher: Take your coat off, Lee.

Lee ignores the teacher.

Teacher: Lee I've asked you once already, take your coat off!

Lee: Alright, I heard you.

Teacher: Well, take it off then.

Lee: I will if you give me a chance. You're always going on at me. What about her? She hasn't got her coat off. You always have a go at me.

Teacher shouts very loudly: Lee, take your coat off and shut up. I'm sick of you whining on.

Lee mutters under his breath something rude, just audible.

Teacher: Get out.

Lee: Why? What did I say?

Teacher knows it was rude but does not know exactly what he said.

In this example, the teacher made the mistake of also being rude to Lee. This is not a model of assertive behaviour. During the Game, the angrier the teacher got, the more it justified Lee's belief that he was being picked on. At the end of the Game the teacher felt frustrated and angry because they did not know exactly what Lee said and therefore could not prove Lee was being rude. Lee of course denied he was being rude. He was able to manipulate the situation and maintain his false belief that teachers picked on him.

Joining in these Games with pupils often results in the teacher losing because these pupils may well argue with every teacher they meet. These pupils are experts in involving teachers in arguments that are irrational.

It would have been much better to start the lesson and then quietly ask Lee to take his coat off. Another method might be to say, 'Lee, all the other pupils have got their coats off, can you now take your coat off, please? Thank you.'

TEACHERS PLAYING GAMES

Teachers themselves may well have their own favourite Games. Some teachers play Persecutor; however well the class works or behaves, the teacher finds something to complain about. Other teachers may play 'I'm helpless'. They constantly complain about a class but, when offered advice, respond with 'Yes but'.

Another game is: 'If it weren't for you...' Here the teacher endlessly moans on about how the class stops them from teaching but does not actually do anything to improve the situation. They start off as a Victim but if they rage at the class they may end up as a Persecutor. This is a teacher version of the Game 'Poor Me'.

ACTIVITY

Think about what your favourite Game is. Do you play Victim, Persecutor or Rescuer?

TRANSFERENCE

Games have an element of transference about them. Transference can clearly be seen in classrooms even in secondary schools when pupils call the teacher 'mum'. Pupils do not see you as an individual and may put the face of another individual on to you, such as one of their parents. Brian may not have been reacting in the here and now, but may have been reacting to his own internal stereotyping of how teachers and adults treat him.

In your lesson a pupil may be involved in transferring the face of their angry and intolerant parent on to you. You may end up with the anger that the pupil should have directed at their parent. In TA terms this is called a 'Hot Potato'. Teachers too can get angry and instead of telling the class who should have been the subject of the anger, they rage at some poor individual who upsets them next lesson. Be aware when you are controlling your anger that if you do not release it safely or fail to be aware of it, you may release it inappropriately towards someone else.

By using the strategies outlined in this chapter, a teacher can spot Games and use Strokes, Contracts, Ego States and Modelling in order not to get involved in them. Games are subjective and irrational. They stop open and honest communication. They stop teachers and pupils from developing 'I'm OK, you're OK' relationships. Therefore it is important to make our classroom Game-Free Zones.

The motive behind Games can vary but the purpose of Games is to confuse the teacher, to move them away from the here and now issue.

Chapter 18

Discounting

Unwarily ignoring information relevant to the solution of a problem.
(Stewart and Joines, 1991)

In classrooms, pupils and teachers are constantly faced by problems. In dealing with these problems, they have two options: use the full power of grown-up thinking, feeling and actions to solve the problem; or try to manipulate the world into providing a solution. In the first choice, they become active, whereas in the second choice, they become passive. TA refers to four different types of passive behaviour:

1. Doing Nothing
   Instead of using energy to solve the problem, the person does nothing.
2. Over-adaptation
   The person discounts their ability to act on their own options; instead they follow the options that others want them to.
3. Agitation
   The person shows agitated behaviour, such as nail biting, hair twiddling, finger drumming. They divert the energy and nervousness into one of these actions instead of solving the problem.
4. Incapacitation and Violence
   The person disables themselves in some way (e.g. by illness), so that someone else has to solve the problem. The person releases a burst of energy, directed against themselves (incapacitation) or others (violence) in a desperate attempt to force the environment to solve the problem for them.

ACTIVITY

Think of a subject which you found difficult or failed in at school. How did that make you feel? Did you feel panic? Was your body tense? Did you feel confused? Did you find it difficult to think? Did you feel stupid? Did you decide that you were worthless? Bear in mind that this is how some pupils may feel in your lessons.

ACTIVITY

Now think about how you behaved in reaction to your feelings. Did you try to be invisible and withdraw from the lesson (doing nothing)? Did you do everything you possibly could to please the teacher (over-adaptation)? Did you start to tap your pen (agitation)? Did you truant in order to avoid that lesson (incapacitation)? Did you hit out at somebody (violence)?

All of the above ways of behaving are passive ways of dealing with fear, panic and self-doubt, because they do not help to solve the problem. They discount the problem, the solutions to the problem and the skills which a person may have to deal with the problem. We are sure that you have experienced all these types of behaviour in some way in the classroom, but we hope that this gives you a clearer insight into why pupils may behave in this way. Let us now look at how you can deal with these types of passive behaviour in a positive way in the classroom.

There are four levels at which people discount (ignore reality).

1. Discounting the existence
    The existence of the problem and other options is discounted.
2. Discounting the significance
    The person realises that they can do something, but feels that it will not make any difference.
3. Discounting the possibility for change
    The person realises that there are alternative ways of doing things and that they might get results, but blanks out the possibility that they could actually put them into practice.
4. Discounting personal abilities
    The person is aware of the options, believes that other people could put them into practice, but dismisses their own ability to do so.

Look at the following example from school.

Teacher: Why have you been sent to me, John?

John: I don't know, I didn't do anything. It's him, he's got a bad temper (discounting the existence of a problem).

Teacher: How many times have you been sent out of your lesson, John?

John: How should I know, I don't keep count (discounting the significance of the problem).

Teacher: Well, this is the third time. Do you realise that your parents will be asked in to school to discuss this?

John: They both work. My dad's a lorry driver and I can get a job with him when I leave school.

Teacher: Well this is becoming a big problem and we will need to discuss it with your parents.

John: Can I go back to my lesson now?

Teacher: No, sit down here.

John: I always get sent out. It's him [the teacher] he just doesn't like me. I can't help that (discounting the possibility for change and discounting personal abilities).

The teacher in this example has not given John any options for different ways of how to deal with this conflict. Pupils like John discount their own responsibility in helping to create the problem and their own ability to behave differently.

Let us look at the same situation again, but this time, the teacher challenges John's discounts and offers him options in order to solve the problem.

Teacher: Why have you been sent to me, John?

John: I don't know.

Teacher: You do know. You stopped other people from learning by talking, and by shouting out. (The teacher has made the pupil aware of the *existence* of the problem.) You know that nobody in this school is allowed to stop a teacher from teaching. (The teacher makes the pupil aware of the *significance* of the problem.) Your parents will now be asked to come into school and we will be putting forward to them evidence from a number of teachers that you cannot behave. This could lead to you being excluded. Do you want that?

John: No.

Teacher: Then here are some things you can do to stop that process. Sit down here and list three things that you can do to make a lesson more enjoyable both for the teacher and for yourself. (The teacher makes the pupil aware of *the possibility for change* and the role that he can play in it, using his own *personal abilities*.)

This can be summarised in the following model:

- Make pupils clearly aware of their behavioural problem.
- Make them aware of the consequences of continuing to behave in this way.
- Make pupils aware that they can choose more positive and productive ways to behave in the classroom.

GRANDIOSITY

Whenever something is discounted, grandiosity occurs. As one part of the situation or problem is ignored or minimised (discounted), another part is exaggerated or blown out of proportion (grandiosity).

Students sometimes defend against their own inferiority or weakness in a subject by being grandiose. They behave as if they are brilliant at a subject when they are in fact weak. They discount their difficulties. David once saw a tutor group put themselves in a line depending on how hard they thought they worked. A number of boys who were *not* very hard-working put themselves at the top of the line where hard workers should be (grandiosity) and a number of hard-working girls put themselves at the bottom of the line where the not so hard-working people should be (discounting). These girls discounted how hard they were working and only concentrated on imagined weaknesses. On the other hand, some pupils exaggerated their efforts.

Teachers can also be grandiose by thinking that, for example, if they miss a lesson close to external exams through illness, then the pupils will fail. They discount the pupils' abilities to work or succeed without their help and exaggerate their own importance.

TEACHERS DISCOUNTING

Teachers need to be aware of the danger of discounting groups by giving them easy work or stereotyping everyone in the group as weak or badly behaved. Some teachers discount their own abilities or successes. They are too willing to focus on their weaknesses and fail to celebrate their successes. This often leads to the successful teacher feeling tired, devalued and depressed. After a difficult lesson with a group, teachers often catastrophise what has happened and discount all the good lessons and success they have had with that group.

It is interesting how some pupils may not be bright in your lesson and yet good in another lesson. Another form of this can be when pupils decide to fail themselves before a teacher or an examiner can do so. They give in, discount their own ability and stop trying to learn.

Chapter 19

Winners and Losers

In a battle, the winners and the losers lose. (Buddha)

ACTIVITY

How do you behave when you are in argument? Are you a sulker? Do you give in and later feel angry because your needs were not met? Is your behaviour passive-aggressive? Do you belittle other people in arguments? Think of a time when someone treated you unfairly or belittled you. Have you forgiven them? If this memory upsets you, quickly jot down the feelings you still have about it. Do you still have 'Stamps' that you want to cash in on this person?

WHAT ARE STAMPS?

Berne developed the concept of Stamps to explain how, instead of solving a problem with Adult awareness, some people collect bad feelings and emotions and then use these to solve the problem. Remember Beth, from Chapter 17. She had been storing up bad feelings about rejection and not being right for over a year and finally she had her pay-off. She feels rejected and she has made the teacher feel bad.

How can we stop pupils from collecting Stamps?

The answer to this question is that basically we cannot. However, we can encourage them to find more productive ways of expressing their thoughts and emotions by modelling and teaching them more open methods of communication. We can create an atmosphere in our classrooms in which it is difficult to collect Stamps because the ethos in the classroom is one of fairness.

We want to help pupils to be 'I'm OK, you're OK'. As teachers, we should aim to create situations in our classroom that can allow everyone to feel like a winner. We need to be aware of students collecting Stamps and then using them to gain their pay-off. There are a number of things we can do in order to resolve conflict quickly and fairly as shown in Table 19.1.

What teachers need to do	Why they need to do it
1 Develop good relationships with our pupils	It is more difficult for pupils to be rude to people they have become attached to.
2 Value ourselves and our subject	Pupils understand that no one is allowed to stop learning from taking place.
3 Teach pupils that in conflict there are no winners	You need to show pupils that your aim is for everyone to be OK in your classroom.
4 Be concerned with changing behaviour and not with punishment	Pupils and teachers can get lost in issues to do with punishment instead of the central issue which is changing and improving behaviour.
5 Be assertive and fair	If you operate from the 'I'm OK, you're OK' position, it will be more difficult for pupils to treat you unfairly.
6 Allow pupils to retreat from conflict with their self-esteem intact	If you make fun of a pupil or treat them disrespectfully, then they will store up Stamps and use them against you. They can see that there are escape routes and every argument does not need to be fought out 'to the death'.
7 Use praise to build up self-esteem and to change behaviour patterns in pupils	By using praise we show pupils that we think they are OK. Behaviour will be more easily changed through using praise rather than getting into a power struggle.
8 Get pupils to reflect on and own their behaviour	Pupils will get into the habit of owning their behaviour.
9 Make pupils aware that their bad choices lead to bad consequences (remember you have choices too)	Pupils see that there is a link between their behaviour and bad consequences.
10 Don't hold grudges. Don't collect Stamps	Don't store up Stamps as a teacher. Again, this leads to unnecessary conflict.
11 Separate the behaviour from the individual	Remember that the pupil is still OK as a person, even if you do not like the way they are behaving.
12 Don't give pupils an audience	Pupils want attention. Give them it for positive things. Don't let them 'perform' or 'show off' in front of their friends.
13 Be open to new ideas and be creative with your discipline.	Don't allow your own ideas of how to manage behaviour to become routine and predictable. Keep them alive and active.

Table 19.1   Ideas for helping teachers to keep their rooms a 'STAMP- free' zone

1 Develop Good Relationships

It is easier to manage a pupil's behaviour when we have a relationship with them. We will generally get back from pupils what we put in. Therefore if we are fair, respectful and positive, then we are more likely to be treated in this way by pupils. It is more difficult to be rude to someone with whom you have formed an attachment than someone whom you see as an object, just another nagging teacher (see Chapters 10 and 11, Transactions and Relationships).

2 Value ourselves and our subject

We need to value ourselves in lessons. It is important that we feel OK about ourselves as teachers. We cannot expect pupils to feel good about themselves, unless we are positive about ourselves and the subject we teach. No one has the right to be unfair to us or to speak rudely to us as teachers. We must show pupils how to value our subject. By teaching in a positive and enthusiastic way, we can demonstrate to pupils that our subject is relevant to them and a worthwhile subject to learn. From this position we can decide that no one has the right to stop us from teaching. This encourages us to defend our right to teach by asserting our rights in a non-aggressive way.

The teacher will say, 'No one in this lesson has the right to stop me from teaching or to stop other pupils from learning. Therefore we need fair rules so that everyone, including me, can do their best. Let me underline, everyone, including me, must do their best. I work hard, and you will work hard. If there is a problem we will sort it out at the end of the lesson when there is time. In this lesson we need to use our time in order to learn.' The teacher is making the pupils aware of the main rule in the room. This is a rule for everyone, including the teacher to keep. When pupils misbehave, they are not falling out with the teacher, they are breaking the rule on learning. This distances the teacher from the conflict. It is more difficult for a pupil to draw the teacher into arguments and games that personalise conflict.

This right to teach is not negotiable; it is our right in our classroom. However, this right will be difficult to enforce if we are disrespectful to pupils or unfair.

3 Teach pupils that in conflict there are no winners

Pupils often have a black and white view of conflict: it is about winning or losing. Teachers have to teach pupils that in a classroom when there is conflict, there is no winner. This stance cuts out the competition, the need to win because you are not fighting to prove a point; you are trying to fairly resolve a problem. Often pupils think that the job of a teacher is to be a professional arguer. Emphasise to pupils that if they are being told off, they are losing and if you are not teaching, you are therefore losing. Point out that in this situation no one is winning.

Teacher: Greg, What is my job?

Greg: To teach.

Teacher: What's your job in the lesson?

Greg: To learn.

Teacher: Who is winning here?

Greg: You are.

Teacher: No, we are both losing. You are not learning and I am not teaching.

In the examples of bad behaviour that we have given, we have demonstrated that no one needs to lose. The teacher makes it clear that they want good behaviour so that they can get on with teaching. If you give punishments out too freely, then pupils will get side-tracked into arguing about the punishment and get involved in Game playing. 'It is not fair'; 'I never did it'; 'You always pick on me'; 'Everyone else was doing it.' They will not concentrate on the central issue, their bad behaviour, and what they need to do to change it.

4 Be concerned with changing behaviour and not with punishment

Make it clear to pupils that you are interested in teaching them and not in punishing them.

Teacher: Jenny, tell me how you were unfair to me?

Jenny: I shouted out.

Teacher: I am not interested in punishing you. What do you think I want to do in my room?

Jenny: Teach.

Teacher: So, if you don't want to be punished, what do you need to do?

Jenny: Stop shouting out.

Teacher: Can you promise me that you will not shout out next lesson?

Jenny: Yes.

Teacher: Right, I do not need to punish you. However, if you shout out next lesson, what will happen?

Jenny: I will be punished.

It is a good idea to sort out a script, so that you can keep the transaction short and precise. You might need to think which Ego State would be most productive with different pupils.

With difficult pupils or in cases when you are short of time you might find being in Adult is the best Ego State to be in.

Teacher: Jimmy.

Jimmy: It wasn't my fault.

Teacher: Jimmy, I want you to answer yes or no to my questions. Did you shout out?

Jimmy: Yes.

Teacher: Is your behaviour helping me to teach, I want a yes or no.

Jimmy: No.

Teacher: If you stop shouting and get on with your work, then there will be no need for any punishment.

Very quickly a pupil like Jimmy could divert the discussion into a victim Game of 'everyone gets away with it and I get blamed'. The teacher does not get lost in Jimmy's Game of 'it's not my fault'. They keep Jimmy focused on what he did wrong and how he can put it right.

'Paddy' a prisoner convicted of murder, having undergone an Anger Management course, wrote this:

'Had I realised how important school was, I'd have been more willing to apply myself. But as so often happens, you lose sight of the actual issues and it becomes a battle of wills. What you are arguing about becomes lost' (Hulme, 1999).

When you have a disagreement with a pupil, make sure you are not disrespectful to them. Don't belittle them, don't be personal and don't use sarcasm. Allow pupils to retreat from conflict with some self-respect. Make them aware that their behaviour is unacceptable, but don't make them feel that they are unacceptable as people. Do not attack their self-esteem. If you don't do this, then they will collect Stamps and then cash them in.

5 Being assertive and fair

It is useful to tell classes: 'I will never be unfair to you, however, no one in this room is allowed to be unfair to me.' It is important that when a teacher has behaved fairly, they do not feel like the loser in the conflict. If they leave a situation with a pupil and still feel angry or resentful, it is likely that they will release their anger or frustration in an inappropriate manner.

Be prepared to say sorry when you are unfair. It is important that when we have been unfair we aim to heal the situation as soon as possible. This might involve you using a non-teaching period to get a pupil out of another teacher's class in order to apologise to them for your unfairness. David has done this and found that pupils sometimes react very sensitively. For example, one pupil he apologised to said, 'It's ok, sir, I could see you were under pressure.' This type of transaction creates more warmth between pupil and teacher and it helps both to feel that they are OK.

This creates a double bind. You are making it clear to pupils that you will never be unfair to them, however, you are also making it clear to them that you will not allow them to be unfair to you. By modelling fairness in your classroom, you are able to demand it as your right.

Teacher: Joe, can you tell me what you did?

Joe: I shouted out when you were trying to explain things to the class.

Teacher: Did this help me, yes or no?

Joe: No.

Teacher: Were you being fair?

Joe: No.

Teacher: Right, you can stop this, by not shouting out and being fair.

We should give pupils an opportunity to be open about their anger or disappointment. In this way they are encouraged not to collect Stamps. Even if they do collect them and try to get a negative pay-off, you can point out that in your lesson they are allowed to talk to you about being unfairly treated.

Creating a time for pupils to discuss problems stops Games such as 'You never listen' and 'I'm always wrong, you're never wrong.' Pupils can be encouraged to talk to the teacher about any problems or resentments at the end of lessons. Emphasise that problems can be sorted at the end of the lesson when there is time to listen carefully and discuss problems.

There are times when you may accuse a pupil of doing something and you are wrong. Make it clear to pupils that you need time to teach and if they feel that they have been unfairly treated then they must see you at the end of the lesson. You can then apologise to the pupil or you might do it publicly in front of the class to model to the class that no one must treat people unfairly in the class, including the teacher.

Teachers can introduce the idea that the teacher does not always expect to be right. As humans we all make mistakes. Therefore the teacher is prepared to apologise when they make a mistake.

6 Allow pupils to retreat from conflict with their self-esteem intact

Give pupils a chance to put a brake on their behaviour.

Teacher: Natalie, at the moment you are going down punishment road. How can you stop this from happening?

Natalie: By getting on with my work and not messing about.

Teacher: Right, do that now.

Give pupils a way out of the trouble. Remember you want to change the behaviour and not punish them.

Teacher: John, just stop for a minute. Take a deep breath and think about this situation before it gets worse.

Here, you are getting John to think about how he can repair the situation rather than allowing him to invest his energy into rebelling or thinking up excuses for his behaviour.

Another method is to use a kind of 'rewind' technique.

Teacher: John, you are heading out of this room. Now you can rewind the situation and put things right by picking up the pen.

7 Use praise to build up self-esteem and to change behaviour patterns in pupils

Many pupils have argument after argument with teachers during the day and will stereotype all teachers as naggers or nasty people who never treat them fairly. These pupils have switched off all channels of communication. We need them to listen to us if we are to alter their behaviour. If we feel someone likes us or has some respect for us, then we are more likely to listen to them.

Choose something that you like about a pupil or something that they have potential to become or do: 'Frank, I know you can be mature, I have seen it in your drama lessons'; 'Marie, I know from Mrs Davies that you can cooperate'; 'I know you are clever'; 'I have seen nice qualities in you.' What you are doing in these examples is to move the pupil from a not OK position to an OK one.

Pupils who get into conflict often do not have a very good self-image. They often have little self-respect for themselves. So before you demand respect from them, you have to move them away from self-hatred.

Make pupils aware of their potential as learners

Teacher: Harry, out of 10, where would you put yourself in terms of intelligence?

Harry: 8.

Teacher: So you see yourself as a clever person?

Harry: Yeah.

Teacher: Where would you put your behaviour?

Here Harry is being forced to say a low number or he is undermining his own view of his cleverness.

Harry: About 4.

Teacher: Is that acceptable for a boy of your intelligence?

Harry: No.

You might have a Harry who says that his intelligence is 4: 'I have been teaching for two years. I know what a clever pupil is like. You are clever. I would double your score at least. I cannot have clever pupils behaving like that.'

Give pupils the opportunity to stop the bad behaviour. 'Terry, at the moment your behaviour is only 5. In my room I expect pupils to be on 7. I am giving you 5 minutes to improve your behaviour.' This technique is also useful for getting pupils to think about how their behaviour will affect their future.

Teacher: In two years you will be leaving school. What mark would you give your behaviour out of 10?

Terry: 4.

Teacher: If you were an employer, would you give someone a job who cannot be behave?

Terry: No.

Teacher: We need to think of ways that you can get your score up to at least 7.

Pupils are encouraged in this process to start to take a long-term view of how their behaviour will limit their prospects after they have left school.

8 Get pupils to reflect on and own their behaviour

When a pupil misbehaves, ask them what it was that they did which got them into trouble. This makes pupils reflect on their own behaviour and own it. Bearing in mind that every piece of behaviour is a form of communication, you might also ask, 'What is it that you want?' or 'What are you trying to achieve here?'

David Button, a teacher with whom David teaches, uses numbers as a way of getting pupils to judge how important an issue was. For example:

Teacher: Out of 10, how important is this?

Pupil: About 2 out of 10.

Teacher: Is it worth getting into an argument and then getting a punishment?

Pupil: Not really.

This is a useful technique because it makes the teacher aware of how important the issue is for the pupil. The teacher might think it's only '3' when the pupil may feel it's '10'. Teachers can use this technique when they feel they are stressed as it helps them to put the issue into perspective.

9 Make pupils aware that their bad choices lead to bad consequences

If punishments have to be given, it is important that pupils are made aware of the consequences of their behaviour and given choices. Pupils need to realise that sanctions and punishments are not just the whim of the teacher or things that vary according to the teacher's mood. We have to be consistent.

Pupils need to realise that sanctions and punishment are a result of their bad choices. This makes it harder for them to shift the teacher into the 'They are not OK' position. It also makes the punishment not something that comes from the teacher but actually arises from their own behaviour. Teacher: 'If you continue to disrupt the lesson, you will end up being punished.' At this moment in time in the conflict, keep the punishment vague. What you want them to hear are the choices. If you start spelling out the punishment, some pupils will get defensive or argumentative about the particular punishment. The teacher continues, 'At the moment you have choices. You can behave or you can continue to misbehave and be punished. Which choice are you going to make?' Make the pupil aware that they have made the wrong choice and make them aware what the consequences of that choice is and who is responsible.

> Teacher: Erica, you have a choice, behave or be punished. At the moment you look like you will lose your break. Who is the person deciding that they do not want a break?

> Erica: You.

> Teacher: No, you are choosing to behave badly. Start making the right choices. Stop talking and complete your work in 15 minutes.

Make pupils aware that their right to have a choice in your lesson is limited.

> Teacher: Matthew, at the moment you have the choice, do you want to stay in my lesson or be sent to the Head of Year?

> Matthew:Stay in the lesson.

> Teacher: You either behave or you no longer have a choice and I will decide.

10 Don't hold grudges and don't collect Stamps

As a teacher, have you ever put up with bad behaviour and not confronted an individual or class only to find yourself at some later date raging at the class or individual over some minor thing? If you've done this, then you have collected Stamps and then cashed them in to get a negative feeling.

ACTIVITY

Try to remember the scenario. What happened? How did you feel? What was your negative pay-off?

Teachers need to model and to teach pupils how to resolve conflict fairly. Before we can teach this to someone else, we need to learn how to do it ourselves.

Look at the example below and think about the teacher's approach to the bad behaviour. Why is it going to encourage conflict rather than resolving it?

Paul comes into the room and leans back on his chair. Last lesson Paul and his teacher had an argument.

Teacher: You've not been in the room more than a minute and you're doing it again.

Paul: What?

Teacher: Don't what me. I have had enough of you're rudeness, lad. Try switching your brain on. You're leaning back on a chair and if you break it, you will pay for it. You're not coming in my lesson telling me what I can and cannot do, get out.

Paul should not have been leaning back on his chair, however, the way the teacher reacted to him was not in the here and now. The teacher was continuing the conflict he had last lesson with Paul.

A better way of dealing with this would be to say: 'Paul, don't lean back on your chair, please. Remember that you could fall and hurt yourself or break the chair and I do not want either of those two things to happen.' It is important as a teacher not to hold grudges or to allow anger to build up and then rage at a class or individual.

We should learn to forgive, if not forget. Aim to start off each new lesson afresh. If a pupil or a class has treated you unfairly, then resolve the situation so that you feel you have been treated fairly. It is important that you can put a full stop at the end of conflict and start again with classes or individuals.

We can shout at someone and it might have an effect, but in the end it will not change behaviour. While we are around the pupil or while we are putting pressure on the pupil, it will work but what we want to do is to help pupils develop their own self-discipline. There are some pupils who react to shouting by getting more aggressive and entrenched in their own irrational views and behaviour. Bring conflict to an end as soon as possible. It is important that we do not hold grudges as teachers.

11 Separate the behaviour from the individual

Make pupils aware that they are OK but their behaviour is not. We have the right not to like the behaviour of a pupil, however, the pupil needs to feel that as a person they are OK. Many pupils will discount their behaviour by saying, 'Mr So and so does not like me. He always picks on me. He didn't like my sister and he is now picking on me'.

By concentrating on their behaviour and not being judgmental about the pupil, the teacher does not push the pupil into an I'm not OK Life Position. The pupil does not have to defend him or herself; they are not personally being attacked. The teacher focuses on the behaviour. The pupil now has to address this and can no longer get into Game playing.

You may be thinking of a particular pupil and be saying to yourself 'but X is a little pain'. The problem with seeing the pupil as a person as not OK, is that once we think this and accept it, then we behave accordingly.

12 Don't give pupils an audience

Pupils with low self-esteem will want to get attention and recognition for their bad behaviour from their peers. If a pupil speaks to you rudely, we would suggest that you ask them politely and calmly to leave your room. Teacher: 'Gail, you have been unfair to me. I want you to stand outside the door, so that we can deal with this problem fairly. At the moment, I am not angry.'

If you had shouted at Gail, the chances are she would have refused to move or she would have shouted back at you. With major confrontations, do not allow pupils to show off or be disrespectful to you in front of the class. It is a good idea to get Gail out of the room. We are aware of the legal problems with leaving a class. However, here we are talking about leaving the classroom door open while you quickly speak to a pupil. Teacher: 'Gail, have I done anything to upset you?' The aim is to take the wind out of Gail's sails. She was probably wound up ready to explode. By not shouting, the teacher has taken Gail by surprise. She is off balance and not sure where the transaction with the teacher is leading. The teacher is also recognising Gail's anger, so she is now less likely to get angry. Gail might say yes or no.

Teacher continues: 'Gail, you know the rule in this classroom, if you are angry with me and I am wrong, then at the end of the lesson I will apologise. But no one is allowed to stop me from teaching. You can either come back into the room and behave or you will be sent to the head of department.' The confrontation is between Gail and the teacher. Other pupils on the edge of trouble have not been allowed to join in. Gail has been isolated and is less sure about herself than she might have been with the backing of one or two of her friends.

If a pupil refuses to leave the room, then there are a number of things which a teacher can do, depending on the situation:

- Tell the pupil that you want them to leave the room so you can discuss the problem privately. Emphasise that there is no punishment involved.
- Check that the pupil understands the serious nature of their refusal by asking 'are you refusing to leave the room?' This gives them a chance to think about what they are doing.
- Send for a more senior colleague.

In extreme situations, for example, if a colleague cannot come, or the pupil is being violent, etc., then you may need to move the whole class and leave the pupil on their own, informing the school office or the senior management team.

13 Be open to new ideas and be creative with your discipline

The very fact that you are reading this book suggests that you are open to trying out new ideas. Treat behaviour management as you would your own subject. Whenever there are new ideas around, be prepared to try some out. If you stick to the same tried and trusted familiar pattern (which can be very effective) the following things may happen:

- Pupils will get used to it and may start to challenge it.
- It may not work for some pupils.
- You will get bored!

When there are winners and losers, there is always a chance for either the teacher or the pupils to collect Stamps. Therefore the strategies outlined in this chapter offer a way for conflict to be resolved quickly and fairly so that no one needs to feel defeated or resentful. Energy in the classroom is then used where it should be, that is in learning, and not in conflict.

Chapter 20

Punishments

Prevention is better than cure.

(Erasmus, 1509)

If teachers consistently use the ideas put forward in this book, then there should be no need to 'punish' pupils because the techniques and strategies advocated are about preventive approaches to disruption. We also feel that the use of rewards (Strokes) should far outweigh the use of punishments given. The power of praise must not be under-rated. Punishment should be a last resort.

When pupils misbehave, teachers often talk about punishing them. The word punishment implies someone suffering for an offence which they have committed. Schools now tend to use the word sanctions instead. This can be either the reward or penalty given for compliance with or non-compliance with a rule or law. This at least has positive as well as negative connotations.

We believe that compensation is a better word to describe what we want from pupils. The pupils make amends for what they have done. They put the situation right. This approach teaches them how to move from a not OK to an OK Life Position. It is also important that pupils are made aware of the implications of bad behaviour outside of the school. This is not just about education in a school setting, but education for life. This ties in with Citizenship.

Any sanction used should link in with the three philosophical assumptions of TA:

- It should make pupils think.
- It should keep them OK.
- It should be about changing behaviour.

In addition, we believe the following should also apply:

- The sanction should be immediate (otherwise the pupils forget what they have done!).
- It should be conducted by the person against whom the offence was committed (another teacher may get the pupil to behave but then the pupil has to go back into the classroom with the original teacher).
- It should be the right offender! (it is better not to punish anyone than to get the wrong person!).

- It should not be enforced on a whole class (they will become resentful towards you).
- It should stress the element of choice in how the pupils behave (bad behaviour does not just happen to them, they have a part to play and can change their decision).
- There should always be a Stroke before the punishment (Rashid, you are normally a polite and hard-working boy so I am disappointed that…).

Below is a list of punishments which are often used. We have separated these into ones we think are OK and ones which are not.

Any punishment that makes amends for the offence committed is considered OK. For example, if a pupil has dropped litter, it would seem appropriate for them first of all to be asked why it is a problem (make them think) and then to be given the task of picking up litter. Similarly, a pupil who writes graffiti on materials or equipment should be asked about what is wrong with what they have done and then given the task of removing the graffiti.

In the classroom, a pupil who continually disrupts the lesson by talking to the person next to them should be given a couple of warnings and then moved to a different seat. Again, they should either be given an explanation of why they have been moved or asked why they think they have been moved. If the problem continues, they may be sent out of the room or sent to another teacher (arranged in advance).

Some teachers use the method of writing a pupil's name on the board when they talk out of turn and adding ticks when they disrupt the lesson again. The idea being that if they get three ticks, then they stay behind in detention. We have found the pupils often turn this into a game, seeing how many ticks they can get. It also gives them an audience and in some cases, gives them self-esteem for misbehaving.

A method which Sandra used was to have a piece of paper in her hand and tell pupils that if they talked out of turn, their name would go on the paper. However, if they then did something 'good' such as answering a question, helping another pupil, being polite or assisting with equipment, then the tick would be erased. This gave them the opportunity to be responsible for their actions and to change and make amends for their misdemeanour.

A similar situation occurs if sanctions are written up on posters in the room. This works with rewards, but with sanctions, again, pupils use it as a kind of test or game. Can they get on to the next level? Will the teacher go through with it? This takes away from the teacher the flexibility to deal with each situation appropriately. It gives them a straitjacket. Having said this, as we have mentioned before, teachers should be clear about what behaviour is acceptable and the possible consequences of bad behaviour. 'Children need consistency. The poor little devils don't know *how* to behave unless they know the limits of what's tolerated and what isn't' (Skynner and Cleese, 1989).

Having a pupil on report seems to have a positive effect. For each lesson, the teacher gets a chance to comment or tick boxes about the way the pupil has behaved, worked and applied him/herself in the classroom. A good way of using this is to keep reminding the pupil during the lesson that they are on report. This should not be done in a threatening way so that the report is used as a stick with which (metaphorically) to beat the pupil. This will set up confrontation and give the pupil no chance to improve. It can be used as a carrot instead. By checking out with them how they think they are behaving, they can be given the opportunity to change and improve and get a good report.

Teacher: Wayne, I see that you are on report for lack of effort today. Give yourself a mark
out of 10 for effort at the moment.

Wayne: 5.

Teacher: If that continues, what do you think I will write on your report?

Wayne: That I wasn't working hard.

Teacher: OK, let's see if you can get up to 9, then I can write some positive things on your
report.

We have even known pupils (particularly boys) ask to be put on report so that they can work hard without losing face in front of their friends or to gain attention This is a clear sign that they are not getting enough positive Strokes.

One way of dealing with a variety of offences is to follow this procedure:

- Get pupils to write down what they have done wrong.
- Ask them to consider why it is wrong, perhaps prompting them with questions about the effect on property, other people, the learning process, etc.
- Get them to write down what they can do to put it right.
- Ask them to make a list of what kind of behaviour will avoid this situation in the future.
- Ask them to sign and date the piece of paper and keep it for future reference.

This ties in with the idea of Contracts.

If pupils are violent, then they need to be taught ways to express their anger safely. Schools have little time to provide special anger management courses, but this would help considerably. One way of dealing with this is through the teaching of PS(H)E (Personal, Social and Health Education). It will also help to equip them with appropriate skills for coping in society.

Another way of dealing with bad behaviour towards others is to aim to develop the pupils' empathy. Sandra experienced a situation when teaching on a split site school when she was verbally abused by a large group of boys on the walk between two sites. Confronting the boys at the time led to them becoming even more abusive and Sandra was left feeling helpless. These were boys with whom, on an individual basis and as pupils in her classroom, Sandra had previously had good relationships.

With the help of Ryan Jervis (a senior teacher), each of the boys involved was identified and spoken to individually. Sandra then had all the boys come to her classroom, sat them at individual desks with a piece of paper, explained to them how she felt about the incident and then asked them to recount the incident in writing. They had to do this from her perspective, right from the moment she left one site of the school to the incident and afterwards. They were also asked to imagine what feelings might have been involved and to write them down. The accounts were remarkably sensitive. After the incident, Sandra held no grudges, the boys were extremely polite and there was no recurrence.

This incident also emphasises the bravado which pupils develop when in a large group or when they have an audience. Hence internal isolation in school can have a very powerful effect. Isolation involves a pupil's being taken out of lessons for a whole day or more, given work to do and supervised by a member of staff throughout. They are not allowed to meet up with their friends at break or to eat their lunch with the rest of the pupils. In addition, if they go to the toilet, they are accompanied and may not go when other pupils have a break. Pupils hate this. Therefore it is an ideal opportunity to get them to really think about the consequences of their behaviour and what they can do to put the situation right. It is the perfect situation in which to teach them techniques and strategies for how to improve and the fact that if they continue to misbehave, they are *choosing* to be isolated.

Punishments that are considered not OK are as follows. First of all, writing out lines hundreds of times. It is mindless, dehumanising and it does not ultimately solve the problem. We should be teaching pupils to do positive and worthwhile tasks. Nor is it good role modelling.

Second, extra work. This means that pupils associate work with punishment and it puts them off learning, which should be enjoyable. It can also make pupils who are already disaffected even more so. Having said this, it seems reasonable to ask pupils to copy up work they have missed or not done due to bad behaviour or if they have not met an important deadline for coursework.

Finally, the ever popular detention. In this next section, by detention, we do not mean individual class teachers keeping pupils behind for a few minutes at the end of the lesson or having them come back to discuss their behaviour at lunchtime, we mean the whole school detention system. This has many disadvantages:

- It brings together all the pupils who have been badly behaved (an audience).
- It is often not immediate (pupils forget what they did).

- It often involves copying out rules or chunks out of a book (which does not help to improve their behaviour).
- It is sometimes conducted by another person (who may not have had any involvement with the offence so pupils dissociate from it).

The RAISE group of pupils were asked about punishments and they felt that the worse punishments were: a letter to their parents or isolation. They considered detentions 'a joke'.

Finally, when punishing a pupil, it is useful to consider the 'shame' element involved. When telling a child off, parents and teachers often say 'you should be ashamed of yourself'. This aspect needs to be handled carefully. Shame is a healthy human emotion. It teaches us our limits and helps us to keep boundaries. It also helps us to see that it is human to make mistakes and that we may need help in putting them right. However, it can also be very destructive. If, for example, the pupil thinks that it is not what they have done which is shameful, but them as a person. This emphasises once again the need to separate the behaviour from the person.

Bradshaw (1988) writes about two forms of shame: 'nourishing shame and toxic/life-destroying shame'. It is the latter which we as teachers should avoid. Bearing in mind some of the negative messages which pupils may have had at home, we at least should give them the opportunity to feel OK about themselves as people and able to change.

Part 5
Staying OK

Chapter 21

How Teachers Can Stay OK

There is no doubt that teaching is a stressful job. In a recent piece of research, teachers and nurses came out 'Top of the League' in terms of stressful jobs. The reasons that it is so stressful are:

- You have to use many different skills.
- You have to deal with lots of different types of people.
- You cannot have a break when you need/want it.
- You have to prepare, write, organise, perform and evaluate several lessons in a day.
- You have external pressure from parents, outside agencies, OFSTED and the government.
- There are always new initiatives being introduced.

Many teachers work long hours in order to give their pupils the best deal and are highly self-critical. This also leads to stress and illness. Buddhist teachings consider that in a 24-hour day, people should have the following:

- 8 hours of work
- 8 hours of play (leisure)
- 8 hours of sleep.

It would seem sensible to use these as a general guide to physical and psychological well-being.

It is important that if we as teachers want to help pupils to feel OK, then we need to nurture and look after ourselves. If teachers feel tired, dispirited or burnt out, then it will be impossible for them to have the energy, awareness and sense of purpose that are needed for many of the ideas discussed in this book to work. With difficult pupils, a teacher needs energy in the classroom. Below are some ideas for teachers to use to look after themselves so that they are not overworking.

- Be aware of your strengths as well as your weaknesses.
- Celebrate successes.
- Accept praise. Don't dismiss praise. Learn to say thank you.
- Produce your own contracts so you are aware of what you want to achieve – time, cost and the benefits.

- Have some fun – laugh.
- Do not catastrophise situations – everyone has bad lessons. In moments of stress, think about whether this will be important in a year's time.
- Remember everyone fails. Learn from failure and become a stronger person. Remember failure may be seen at a later date as preferable to success.
- If you feel stressed, do something to release your stress. Use exercise, visualisation techniques, Tai Chi, Yoga or meditation.
- Give yourself time each day just for you.
- Remember to breathe. During the course of a day, stop and breathe. Make sure your breathing is not shallow; breathe from your stomach.
- Make sure you get enough sleep.
- Eat properly – fresh fruit and vegetables.
- Don't drink too much alcohol.
- Remember that you get what you focus your mind on.
- Don't continually moan about things. Think positively, look for solutions.
- Be positive; concentrate on what you want to happen.
- Be flexible. Be prepared to change and try new ideas out.
- Go on courses so that your teaching improves and you feel stimulated and interested in your job.
- Discuss problems with colleagues and get advice.
- Remember pupils with behavioural problems will be a problem with most teachers. If some teachers do not have problems with an individual, find out what they are doing.
- Be organised. Decide what your priorities are each week.
- Keep a log of the hours you are working. If you are working too hard, stop.
- Learn to say no. Do not agree to take on more work just to please other people.
- Don't work through your breaks or dinnertime.
- Remember 'I *have* a job but I *am not* that job'.
- Develop your own positive affirmations so that you can keep your energy and spirits up.
- Be realistic about the targets you set yourself. Don't try to be more than human.
- Get plants for your room. If they are dying, then this is a sign you are not nurturing or looking after yourself.
- Be aware of your Driver behaviour – Be perfect, Please others, Try hard, Be strong, Hurry up. You may need to see a counsellor or psychotherapist to work on giving yourself permission not to be driven by these limiting beliefs.

In a time when assessment, examinations and league tables are seen as important, pupils also get stressed. If teachers stay OK, then they can teach pupils to do the same. In other words, it is good role modelling.

At the time of writing, much is being said in the media about the shortage of teachers and the lack of good teachers. 'Shortage could last forever' (Nic Barnard writing in *The Times Educational Supplement* 31 August 2001). This is thought to be due to:

- recruitment problems (many graduates do not consider teaching as an option)
- retention problems (many teachers leave the job within the first three years)
- retirement problems (over the next decade, more and more teachers will be reaching retirement age).

Our feelings are that although money is an issue, it is the workload and the constant daily pressure which make teaching stressful. Pupils are not like paperwork in an 'In Tray' which can be pushed aside and dealt with later, they are 'in your face'. Teachers need time out of the classroom in order to do the following:

- prepare lessons thoroughly
- mark work
- familiarise themselves with new examinations and initiatives
- devise new resources,
- do their administrative work effectively
- reflect on what they are doing
- develop new ideas for motivating pupils
- read
- share their experiences and concerns with other teachers.

It is important that teachers stay OK in order to be able to encourage pupils to move to being OK.

Chapter 22

Conclusion

Managing behaviour is a challenge for all teachers. Whatever your experience as a teacher, there will always be difficult individuals, groups or situations to deal with. Often there are no magical solutions to these problems. However, throughout this book we have suggested that managing behaviour is easier when teachers have developed a relationship with pupils.

The ideas we have put forward are not meant to be prescriptive, but rather a framework for teachers to use in order to:

- recognise certain types of behaviour
- understand what is happening and why
- develop strategies for dealing with it.

We have shown that there are positive and pro-active things that teachers can do. These are:

- Respect pupils and realise that they have the potential to be OK.
- Move pupils to the OK Life Position.
- Keep communication channels with pupils open.
- Give pupils responsibility for their own learning.
- Use praise rather than punishment.
- Be aware of your own behaviour and model OK behaviour.
- Avoid conflict if possible and resolve it quickly and fairly.

These ideas provide you with alternative ways of approaching discipline. The emphasis is very much on developing awareness. It is also important to note that behaviour management is not just about changing the behaviour of pupils but also that of teachers. Throughout the book we have made it clear that teachers need to help pupils to develop their social and emotional skills as well as their intellectual potential in school.

Many pupils who do not feel OK about themselves have little or no self-respect or self-esteem. When working with disaffected pupils, there have often been moments when we have noticed a shift in a pupil's behaviour. There is a change in the way the pupil perceives themselves and their relationship with us. Something triggers this move to an I'm OK Life Position. It might have been a smile from us, praise, the pupil's own sense of achievement, the feeling they have been listened to and valued, or a combination of all of these. It has been these moments that have inspired us to write this book. Hopefully, this book will encourage you to develop your own ideas and strategies to encourage pupils to feel OK.

Appendix 1 Class Contract

OUR AGREEMENT

I agree to the rules below because they will help the class to have good lessons

1. We must listen to the teacher when they are talking to the whole class.

2. We need to put our hands up if we want to be heard by the rest of the class.

3. We must talk quietly to each other.

4. We should get on with our work and do our best.

5. We should talk politely to............and to each other.

6. We have to do our homework (it will help our learning).

7. We will talk to........about any problems at the end of the lesson.

8. We will say sorry when we are unfair to other people.

Signed by...Date.................

Appendix 2 Behaviour Contract

Behaviour Contract

Teacher: Mr/Ms _____ Pupil _____

No one in Mr/Ms _____ lessons is allowed to stop him/her from

teaching or prevent other pupils from learning.

What I have done wrong in lessons?

In Mr/Ms _____ lesson I have been unfair and prevented him/her

from teaching by

_____

_____

_____

How I can put this right?

I can stop being unfair in lessons by _____

_____

_____

_____

My targets are:

1 _____

2 _____

3 _____

What will be the benefits of behaving?

Improving my behaviour will help me to avoid getting into trouble.

It will also help me _____

_____

By behaving fairly I will improve my learning, get more rewards and enjoy the lesson more.

If I continue to behave badly, the following things will happen:

_____

_____

_____

I _____ agree to honour this contract and I am now

fully aware of the consequences of breaking the contract.

Signed _____ Witnessed by

Date _____

Appendix 3 Certificates

Certificates to hand out at the end of language lessons. These would all be in different colours with pictures on them. They are A5 size. Pupils have a reduced copy of all of them in their books, so they can tick off which ones they have got. There are also posters on the walls.

An excellent piece of homework	Good behaviour in class
Linguist of the day	Lovely accent
Good effort in languages	Quality language work
Best improver	(Insert your own certificate here)

Appendix 4 Letter to Parents

Dear

In the Modern Languages Department, we regularly reward pupils in class by awarding certificates to them at the end of each lesson. There are seven different certificates which a pupil can be given. They read as follows:

Good effort in languages
Quality language work
Linguist of the day
Good behaviour in class
Best improver
An excellent piece of homework
Lovely accent

When a pupil collects any three certificates, s/he gains a merit certificate which is awarded in assembly.

I am pleased to inform you that your son/daughter ……………………………….
of form …………… has managed to earn all seven certificates.

This clearly shows a keen interest in the subject, a conscientious approach to homework, good behaviour in class and excellent language skills.

We are delighted with his/her work and hope that s/he will continue to adopt this positive approach next year.

Yours sincerely,

Ms S. Newell
Head of Modern Languages   Head of Year

Glossary of TA Terminology

Adapted Child	Using the Child Ego State to fit in with other people or society.
Adult Ego State	Behaviour, thoughts and feelings in response to what is happening in the moment.
Agitation	Repetitive, purposeless behaviour which does not solve the problem.
Child Ego Sate	Behaviour, thoughts and feelings repeated from when the person was actually a child.
Complementary Transaction	A transaction in which the vectors are parallel. The Ego State which responds is the one which was addressed.
Con	A transaction which invites someone psychologically into playing a Game.
Conditional Stroke	Recognition or attention for what you do.
Contract	A commitment made in Adult to yourself or someone else to make a change.
Controlling Parent or Critical Parent	Using the Parent Ego State to criticise or control people.
Counterfeit Stroke	Praise which the person does not mean.
Crossed Transaction	A transaction in which the vectors are crossed. The Ego State which responds is not the one which was addressed.
Cross-Up	The moment of confusion in a Game which is experienced straight after the 'Switch'.
Discounting	Out of awareness, ignoring information which could help to solve a problem.
Drama Triangle	A diagram which shows how people can move between the three positions of Victim, Rescuer and Persecutor.
Driver	One of five ways of behaving which can flag up a person's script.
Egogram	A bar chart on which people can intuitively show how much they use or the importance of each of the Ego States in the functional model.

Ego State	A consistent pattern of feelings and experience which links to a pattern of behaviour.
Frame of Reference	The way a person views and understands themselves, other people and the world.
Free Child	Using the Child Ego State to express wants and needs without censoring them, regardless of rules or the demands of society.
Functional Model of Ego States	How we use the Parent, Adult and Child Ego States.
Game	A series of transactions which follows a set pattern including a Con, a Gimmick, a Switch, a Cross-up and a Pay-off.
Gimmick	A response on the psychological level that means the person is joining in the Game.
Grandiosity	Exaggerating reality.
Incapacitation	Deliberately making sure that you cannot do something yourself in order to solve a problem and forcing someone else or the environment to do so.
Life Position	A person's beliefs about themselves and others which they use to justify their behaviour and decisions.
Life Script	A kind of plan for life made in childhood without realising it, which parents reinforce and which seems to be backed up by events which follow.
Loser	Someone who does not achieve what they want to.
Marshmallow Strokes	Praise which is not genuine.
Negative Stroke	Recognition or attention which is received as being uncomfortable or unpleasant.
Nurturing Parent	How a person uses the Parent Ego State to be nurturing, helpful and caring.
Over-adaptation	Doing what other people want without looking after your needs nor checking that is what people actually want.
Parent Ego State	Behaviour, thoughts and feelings which have been copied from your parents or whoever looked after you as a child.
Passive behaviour	Not doing what is needed in order to solve a problem.
Pastime	Talking about everyday events. Chatting.

Pay-Off	The feeling a person is left with at the end of a Game.
Persecutor	A person who puts other people down.
Plastic Stroke	Praise or recognition which is not genuine.
Positive Stroke	Something which a person says or does to you which feels pleasant.
Rebellious Child	Using the Child Ego State to rebel against rules.
Recognition Hunger	Wanting others to notice you.
Rescuer	Someone who helps when it is not really needed Often done from the 'one up' position.
Ritual	A familiar and repetitive way of doing things or transacting.
Spontaneous	Choosing freely from the many ways of thinking, feeling and behaving, including the right choice of Ego State.
Stamp	A negative feeling which the person remembers and uses against someone later.
Stimulus Hunger	The need for mental and physical stimulation.
Stroke	A unit of recognition.
Structural Model Ego States	The content of the Parent, Adult and Child.
Switch	The point in a Game where the person changes roles so that they can collect their 'Pay-off'.
Time Structuring	How people spend their time when they are in pairs or groups.
Transaction	The basic unit of social discourse.
Ulterior Transaction	A transaction in which there is an explicit and a hidden message.
Unconditional Stroke	Praise or recognition for what or who the person is.
Victim	A person who operates from the 'one down' position where they get belittled or seem unable to manage without help.
Winner	Someone who achieves what they want.
Withdrawal	Not joining in or transacting with other people.

Further Reading

Berne, E. (1963) *Structure and Dynamics of Organisations and Groups.* New York: Random House Company.

Berne, E. (1971) *A Layman's Guide to Psychiatry and Psychoanalysis.* Harmondsworth: Penguin.

Berne, E. (1996) *Transactional Analysis in Psychotherapy.* London: Souvenir Press.

Bradshaw, J. (1991) *Home Coming.* London: Piatkus.

Bradshaw, J. (1993) *Creating Love.* London: Piatkus.

Carlson, R. (1999) *Don't Sweat the Small Stuff at Work.* London: Hodder and Stoughton.

Carlson, R. and Bailey, J. (1998) *Slowing Down to the Speed of Life.* London: Hodder and Stoughton.

Clarkson, P. (1992) *Transactional Analysis Psychotherapy: An Integrated Approach.* London: Routledge.

Culley, S. (1993) *Integrative Counselling Skills in Action.* London: Sage.

De Board, R. (1998) *Counselling for Toads.* London: Routledge.

Dryden, W. (ed.) (1992) *Key Issues for Counselling in Action.* London: Sage.

Goleman, D. (1998) *Working with Emotional Intelligence.* New York: Bantam Books.

Kaufman, G. (1993) *The Psychology of Shame.* London: Routledge.

Kindlon, D. and Thompson, M. (2000) *Raising Cain.* Harmondsworth: Penguin.

Sills, C. (1997) *Contracts in Counselling.* London: Sage.

Smith, M. (1989) *When I Say No, I Feel Guilty.* New York: Bantam Books.

Steiner, C. (1974) *Scripts People Live.* New York: Bantam Books.

Steiner, C. (1997) *Achieving Emotional Literacy.* London: Bloomsbury Publishing.

Stewart, I. (1991) *Transactional Analysis Counselling in Action.* London: Sage.

Stewart, I. (1999) *Developing Transactional Analysis Counselling.* London: Sage.

Tilney, T. (1998) *Dictionary of Transactional Analysis.* London: Whurr.

Wilson, P. (1987) *The Calm Technique.* London: HarperCollins Publishers.

Bibliography

Berne, E. (1973) *Sex in Human Loving*. Harmondsworth: Penguin.

Berne, E. (1984) *Games People Play*. Harmondsworth: Penguin.

Berne, E. (1991) *What Do You Say after You Say Hello?* London: Corgi Books.

Bradshaw, J. (1988) *Healing the Shame that Binds You*. Deerfield Beach, Florida: Piatkus.

Capel, S. Leask, M. and Turner, T. (1999) *Learning to Teach in the Secondary School* (2nd edn). London: Routledge.

Dusay, J. (1977) *Egograms*. New York: Harper and Row.

Ernst, K. (1972) *Games Students Play*. Berkeley, CA: Celestial Arts.

Field, L. (1993) *Creating Self-esteem*. London: Element.

Fisher, R. and Ury, W. (1989) *Getting to Yes*. London: Hutchinson Business Books.

Gardner, H. (1983) *Frames of Mind*. New York: Basic Books.

Gardner, H. (1999) *Multiple Intelligences: The Theory in Practice*. New York: Basic Books.

Goleman, D. (1996) *Emotional Intelligence*. London: Bloomsbury Publishing.

Goulding, M. and Goulding R. (1979) *Changing Lives through Redecision Therapy*. New York: Grove Press.

Harris, T. (1973) *I'm OK – You're OK*. London: Pan Books.

Harris, T. and Harris A. (1986) *Staying OK*. London: Pan Books.

Hay, J. (1993) *Working It Out at Work*. Watford: Sherwood Publishing.

Huber, C. (2000) *How to Get from Where You Are To Where You Want to Be*. Carlsbad, CA: Hay House.

Hulme, C. (1999) *Manslaughter United*. London: Yellow Jersey Press.

Humphreys, T. (1998) *A Different Kind of Discipline*. Dublin: Newleaf.

James, M. (1977) *The OK Boss*. New York: Bantam Books.

James, M. and Jongeward, D. (1996) *Born to Win*. 25th anniversary edition. New York: Perseus Books.

Karpman, S. (1968) 'Fairy tales and script drama analysis', *TAB* 7(26): 39–43.

Karpman, S. (1971) 'Options', *TAJ* (1): 79–87.

Kornfield, J. (2000) *After the Ecstasy, the Laundry*. London: Rider Books.

Kundtz, D. (1998) *Stopping*. Berkeley, CA: Conari Press.

Levin, P. (1988) *Cycles of Power*. Deerfield Beach, Florida: Health Communications Inc.

Lindenfield, G. (1992) *Assert Yourself.* Glasgow: HarperCollins Publishers.

Lindenfield, G. (1993) *Managing Anger.* Glasgow: HarperCollins Publishers.

Lindenfield, G. (1994) *Confident Children.* Glasgow: HarperCollins Publishers.

Millman, D. (1999) *Everyday Enlightenment.* London: Hodder and Stoughton.

Richmond, L. (1999) *Work as a Spiritual Practice.* London: Piatkus.

Samways, L. (1997) *The 12 Secrets of Health and Happiness.* Victoria, Australia: Penguin.

Skynner, R. and Cleese, J. (1989) *Families and How to Survive Them.* London: Methuen.

Steiner, C. (1971) 'The Stroke economy', *TAJ* 1(3): 9-15.

Steiner, C. (1974) *Scripts People Live: Transactional Analysis of Life Scripts.* London: Grove Press.

Stewart, I. (1992) *Eric Berne.* London: Sage Publications.

Stewart, I. and Joines, V. (1991) *TA Today.* Nottingham: Lifespace Publishing.

Tuckman, B.W. (1965) 'Developmental sequence in small groups', *Psychological Bulletin* 63 (6): 384–99.

Woollams, S. and Brown, M. (1978) *Transactional Analysis.* Michigan: Stan Woollams.